ZORAH CHOLMONDELEY
plants, flowers and trees. As a c
outdoors, immersing herself in .... years later, with the discovery of Shamanism and attending Caitlin and John Matthews' 'Walkers Between the Worlds' programme, that she started to receive healing and guidance from Queen Maeve of the Fae. Queen Maeve inspired her to connect with the spirits of plants and trees and Zorah posted the messages she received on her homepage. Zorah holds a monthly circle where participants connect to the spirit of a plant, tree or the fae to receive wisdom, healing and inspiration. Her next project is to create a Lemurian healing garden based on the conscious gardening principles discussed in this book. You can follow her progress on her website zorahhealing.co.uk and related social media.

THE ENCHANTED GARDEN

*Conscious Gardening with the Fae
and Nature's Elementals*

ZORAH CHOLMONDELEY

CLAIRVIEW

Clairview Books Ltd.
Russet, Sandy Lane,
West Hoathly,
W. Sussex RH19 4QQ

www.clairviewbooks.com

Published by Clairview Books 2021

A CIP catalogue record for this book is available from the British Library

ISBN 978 1 912992 28 7

Cover by Morgan Creative
Typeset by Symbiosys Technologies, Vishakapatnam, India
Printed and bound by 4Edge Ltd, Essex

CONTENTS

May the star be at your brow,
may the moon be at your belly,
may the cup be at your feet.
In Nature is truth.
Blessed be.

(Message from the yew tree, as received by Zorah Cholmondeley)

FOREWORD

I am part of the incoming tide of individuals gently waking people up to the consciousness of Nature and Nature's intelligence. If we co-create with Nature spirits and the fae, ours will become a world of infinite possibilities for love, joy and togetherness. We just need to be still for long enough and listen with our hearts to the natural world all around us, whether it be rock, crystal, plant, tree, animal, insect or the subtle world of the fae, Nature spirits, dragons, unicorns.

I have had a fascination for the fae ever since my childhood. I bought the well-known book *Faeries* by Brian Froud and Alan Lee and remember pouring over the beautiful pictures and marvelling at the myths and legends contained within the pages, loving the idea of a magical dimension where the fae resided. It wasn't until my early 30s that I started to feel a presence turn up in my meditations who called herself Queen Maeve of the Fae. She originally showed up in her sovereign, warrior aspect which was totally relevant to my life experiences at that time as I was constantly giving my power away in relationships. Then I started exploring shamanism and journeying, attending Caitlin and John Matthews' 'Walkers Between The Worlds' courses. Shamanic journeying, also called 'spirit flight', is where the shaman travels into other worlds or the subtle reality of the cosmos and meets their spiritual allies who can assume animal or human form. These allies help the shaman to navigate the otherworld to bring back wisdom, healing and inspiration connected to the original intention for the journey. This is facilitated by the rapid beat of a drum which alters the shaman's consciousness so that the otherworld can be more easily perceived. Shamanism allows us to see the interconnectedness of all life and helps us wake up to the importance of the part we play in looking after this beautiful planet.

As I started to venture into the otherworld on my shamanic journeys, Queen Maeve often joined me and started to voice her concerns over the damage humanity was causing to the environment. She introduced me to the concept that a portion of our gardens should be left wild, encouraging and supporting wildlife and forging a closer connection to the fae. From this was born the idea of a book, recording the information being received not only from Queen Maeve and the fae but also other nature beings—including gnomes, dragons and Master Pan, to name just a few. All of them commented on the impact humanity is causing to the environment and outlined a way forward, starting with our gardens. They also explained their individual roles within the complexity of Nature.

This book is for those who love their gardens and gardening and are also committed to their spiritual growth. I introduce the concept of gardens as being a way to connect to our true nature and as a mirror to how we approach life. It is also for those who want to connect to the fae and learn more about them, and for those who want to take better care of the planet through tending to their gardens with more enlightenment.

*

My faery guardian wanted the word 'enchanted' used in the title of this book as she believes it will stir long-forgotten memories within humanity's collective consciousness, to a time when we were enchanted with the world. We were literally in reverence and awe of the world and thus treated it with more respect, and cherished and looked after it.

To explain 'gardening the faery way', she says:

> We will show you how to open up to the consciousness of your garden as a whole and to co-create with the individual Nature spirits and faeries within it as it was in Lemurian times. We wish to bring to your attention the tremendous variety and interplay of non-physical life forms living on and within the earth including the faery races, gnomes and dragons to name just a few, all with a unique part to play in the health of the planet. Together we can co-create a heaven on earth.

The faery realm has long been forgotten and passed into the mists of time, emerging now and again as myths and legends, mainly for our children's entertainment. Now is the time to reconnect and learn from the faery realm how to care for our home. The wake-up call to look after our planet is ringing out all over the world as Mother Earth ascends, carrying us with it. Many souls are departing as they are clinging to the old ways and paradigms that no longer resonate and because they steadfastly refuse to embrace the higher vibration and work with this new level of light. As the earth holds more and more light, it will become easier for those of us who have chosen to ascend with her to connect with the Nature spirits and guardians, including the faery realm for this planet. So, we must relearn how to do this, and the faery realm has stepped forward to be our guide for *gardening the faery way*. This literally means gardening with more enlightenment—being conscious of the energy behind form, the faery behind the plant!

INTRODUCTION: GETTING BACK TO NATURE AND OUR TRUE NATURE

Gardens sing to the soul, stir us to remember who we truly are. They shine the light on our worries, dispelling them and restoring us to harmony. They soothe us, rock us, and enfold us in a blissful blanket of green. They revitalize us when our spirits are low and enthral us when we rest our eyes on a single flower of beauty. Gardens restore us to being right with the world, right with ourselves, resting in our right brain of being-ness and the divine feminine. They remind us that our journey here on earth is as spiritual beings enrobed in physicality.

All land is sacred and should be treated as such. Our gardens are a microcosm within the macrocosm. How we treat our land and the right relationship we foster with it can extend out to others and, indeed, the world.

There are numerous dimensions to a garden, parallel realities over-lapping in a kaleidoscope of colours; the faery realm is one. You may be blessed to have a portal to the faery kingdom in your garden, but whether you have one or not, faeries will visit if they are made welcome, for they want to make a new alliance with us in these historic times of ascension. They want us to tune into Nature on a much deeper level in order to become aware of all of Nature's co-creators in the spiritual realms and to become aware of Gaia herself. Gaia is the soul of Mother Earth. She needs our love, care and attention—especially for the patch of land we call our 'garden', for it is here that we can 're-remember' our duties and responsibilities towards her and the male counterpart of earth's consciousness, Geb.* It is here that we can re-remember our role to play in her ascension and ours.

Lemurian energies also have a part to play within our garden. Lemu-ria was an ancient civilization that existed before Atlantis. We can

---

* See *Messages from Nature's Guardians* by Fiona Murray.

consciously connect with these energies and anchor them into the land. Lemurian energy is one of unconditional love, harmony and oneness; once planted and anchored in our hearts and gardens, it can then spread out to our beautiful planet. The Garden of Eden was the time of Lemuria, a time of peace, love, unity, consciousness and beauty. It was a time of mutual cooperation and honouring of all paths and all lines of evolution, including the angels, faeries, elementals, animal-, plant-, tree- and mineral-kingdoms. Love was the only exchange in these times, the only currency, and instant manifestation of one's heart's desires was everyone's birthright. The Lemurians created things of great beauty for the sheer pleasure and joy they brought. The natural world was revered, honoured and sanctified and gardens were seen as essential for 'right living'.

Our gardens now are a small reminder, a long-forgotten memory of these past times, but they can facilitate a very important step on our evolution back to wholeness and Source.

And so our journey begins…

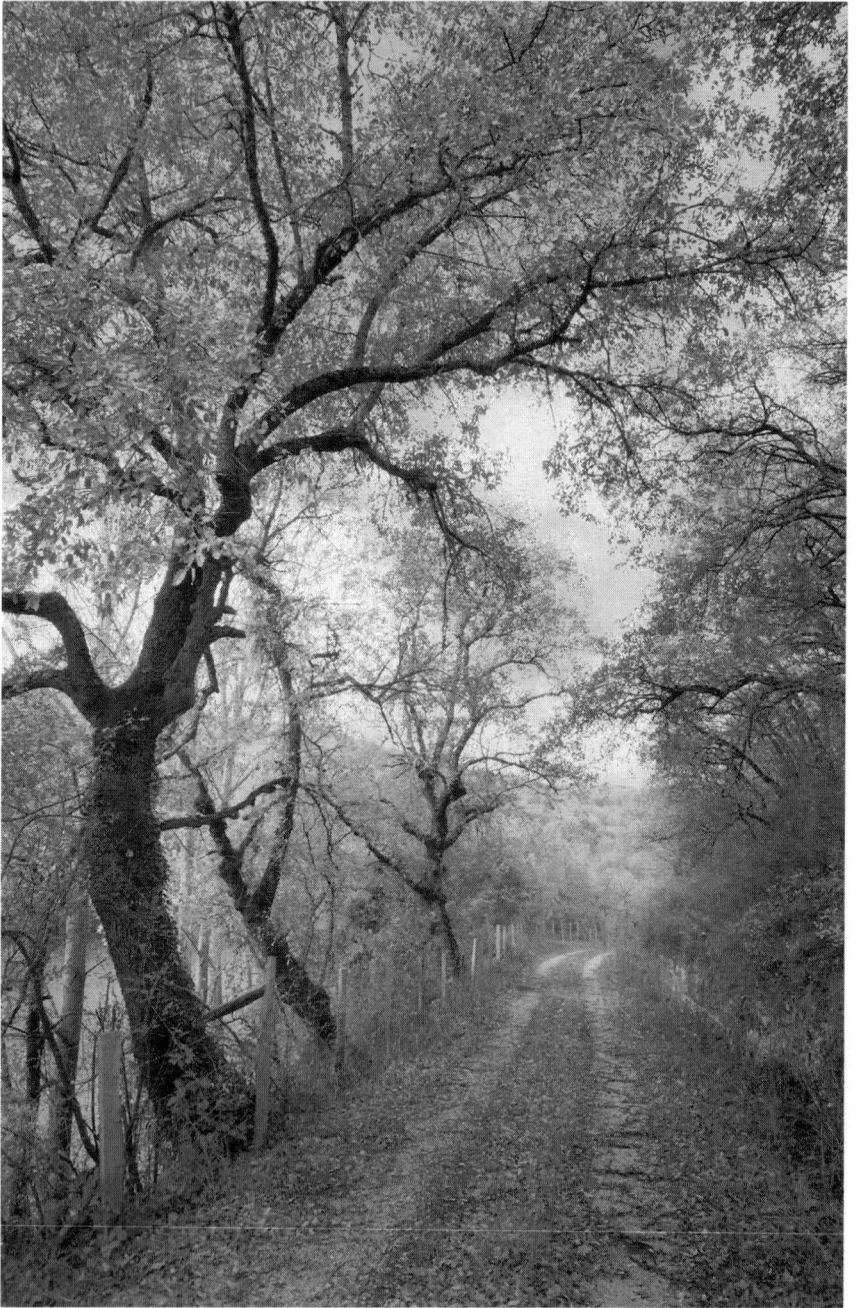

PART ONE:
INTRODUCING A DEEPER REALITY OF NATURE

1. FAERY HISTORY

Once upon a time, a very long time ago, there lived a queen of diaphanous beauty, immense stature and pure love. She ruled her people with stately grace and a firm hand and the world was a richer place, for the fae lived among people. They often made merry and their laughter filled the air, especially on Midsummer's Eve, when celebrations were to be had by all the fae folk.

Human and faery lived side by side in the wondrous cities of Atlantis but more so in the green places of Nature: forests, woods, tree and fell. People would visit the fae for their wisdom and guidance on issues of Nature and the natural world and the fae in turn asked nothing more than to live on the land, side by side with humanity, within the green, wondrous spaces of earth. Indeed, angels also walked with man and imparted their wisdom, and inspired human beings to keep connection with their higher selves. The fae inspired humans to be centred in their true nature. Life was rich and wondrous for humanity at that time, as can only be when there is a mix of life forms.

When human beings fell from grace and grew denser, losing their connection to the finer realms, they became cruel and self-centred and committed many a dark deed born from fear and ignorance.

And the fae? They retreated to the Hollow Hills, the hollow bones of Mother Nature, an alternate dimension. They made their homes there and took all the beauty and sparkle with them, since man could no longer see or appreciate it.

But the fae have waited here for unmeasured time, since fae time is no time...

2. QUEEN MAEVE OF THE FAE SPEAKS

We have waited to reunite with our brothers and sisters of humanity because we believe life will be richer for both of us, and as guardians of Nature and the natural world we are so concerned with what you are doing: ravaging, pillaging, plundering, taking, laying bare the earth, stripping the greenery that is so important for the health and healing of the planet, and indeed for all of mankind.

The time is now for us to return but you must create sacred spaces for us to make forays into your world and connect with your seers. These places in Nature must be wild and dedicated to the fae. Large swathes of land, wild and rugged, are already frequented by us. We see you love your gardens, your little green spaces, where you attempt to reconnect with your true natures through the natural world. We propose a liaison between the fae and yourselves, through dedicated wild spaces in your gardens. They have become too manicured and regimented and the life force is not as strong as it would be in a wild uncultivated place. Certain plants create sacred natural energies, and certain configurations upon the earth, in rock and crystal, create favourable conditions for portals where we as a race can come and go at our pleasure... and it is our vain hope that we will be able to interact with the seers of your realm and forge links into humanity's consciousness, into the closed minds of men.

Your world has become disenchanted. By reconnecting with the faery realm, it is our fondest hope that your people will again see enchantment as fundamental to a more fulfilling way of life. Many of you see life as mundane, full of chaos and tasks and must do's; through this filter your eyes perceive your world as dull and grey—devoid of spirit, colour, adventure. I say to you, this does not have to be so. All that glitters is not gold, but one needs a little glitter to inspire and ignite the heart, to awaken the soul's passion and to take risks for exhilaration and self-fulfilment. Was it not your own poet Dante who did say, 'Beauty awakens the soul to act'? Enchantment is not the same as bewitching. The latter is a form of control, the former a way of seeing—and through enchantment there is a raising of the spirit and a reaching towards your soul's rhapsody.

We wish to walk again with men, women and children to mutually enrich lives, but this does depend on humanity's spiritual evolution, for it is true that dark feelings can completely consume us. If we come into close contact with a human's dark feelings, we can absorb them and become dark ourselves. This is one of the reasons we have sought retreat in the Hollow Hills, away from the dark thoughts of men.

A prerequisite to becoming re-enchanted is to be fully grounded, otherwise one can become 'away with the faeries' and one cannot bring into reality any of the inspiration received.

There is much fear and untruth told about the faery realm and this has been passed down through the ages. The Christian church was a force seeking sole power over man without distraction of enchantment and the fae. So man has woven many lies about us, and there is a whole section of our people who despise mankind and will have nothing to do with you. We hope that by reconnecting with your world we can show them what can be achieved and what unimaginable richness a liaison will bring. But until that day, it is best that they are left well alone.

Who is Queen Maeve?

I posed this question to her and this is what she said:

I am an aspect of the great goddess, she who has many forms, and I am known by the name of Queen Maeve here in the British Isles but have many other names the world over. I came into being when the fae retreated to 'Hollow Earth'—the channel through which humanity could reconnect to the fae, once they had sufficiently raised their consciousness again and wished to return to a heaven-on-earth that we knew and shared so long ago, in earth time. The fae can connect to humanity through me or directly, as they wish. More and more of humanity is waking up and connecting with the subtle realms, as has been foretold, and in doing so I evolve to eventually become part of your consciousness—enabling you to perceive and directly communicate with the fae. Honour me in your gardens and green places and the fae will have a stronger connection to you and your land through my presence. Together we will build bridges and usher in a new dawn of enlightenment.

A year after this was written, in September 2017, after the Lion's Gate* opened and the new codes of light poured onto our planet, Queen Maeve of the Fae now embodies a higher level of light.

All of us are working tirelessly behind the scenes in Nature to usher in the new golden dawn. If you connect with me in heart-centred meditative awareness, and allow me to flow more light into your being and then look at the plants in your garden, you may see that they glow with a light and vibrancy not seen or felt before. Their colours will seem more intense. If you are clairvoyant, you may even see the Nature spirits and elementals at work. This new higher vibrational earth is already here. You just need to shift your frequency to sense it.

I then became aware of the community of the fae celebrating in their great halls, celebrating this new level of light both of Mother Earth and of themselves. They glowed white with soft pink. The fae need this higher level of light in order to be stewards of this new earth.

---

* Lion's Gate is a star portal with this name due to the sun being in the constellation of Leo. This portal is activated once each year when the sun aligns with Sirius. Sirius is believed to hold knowledge and wisdom from higher divine realms and is often referred to as the spiritual sun. When the sun and Sirius meet during the period 26 July to 12 August, their energies intensify and earth is able to receive 'light energy' from both of these celestial bodies. It is at its most powerful on 8 August and helps to raise the consciousness/light of the earth, enhancing spiritual awakenings and bringing new insights and awareness to humanity.

Most recently, as we are fast approaching May Eve 2021, a time when Queen Maeve is most active, I received the following:

> *We are in a new chapter of earth's history—a time of resurrection codes both for the planet and her many realms, including that of humanity. The importance of consulting your heart in all matters cannot be overemphasized. Feelings are the only way to navigate through these times, without which the intellect will lead humanity to a barren wasteland. Listen to the voice of your heart, for this is the voice of your soul and 'I Am'* presence. Put love first with all choices made and never choose from fear.*

I see the Sidhe, a faery race,[†] in white armour upon majestic steeds, pawing at the ground—a metaphor for their being ready for humanity's clarion call. The fae are ambassadors for this New Earth and are waiting to co-create with us. All new ideas and concepts to mitigate further environmental catastrophe have their backing. They and Queen Maeve will come to anyone who calls them, supporting us in our endeavours, however small we perceive our contribution to be.

---

* 'I Am' presence is that which is eternal about us, pure love and wholeness/holiness.

† See chapter 'A bit about faeries'.

3. QUEEN MAEVE'S MEDITATION

Our imagination is a gateway to other spiritual realms. When you use your imagination to find yourself in an inner world, you are creating a special state within yourself which allows you to connect with and perceive other beings of light. So, when your mind tells you that you have fantasized an experience in meditation, know that it is not fantasy but real. It is your fearful ego at work trying to convince you otherwise. Just smile and send your ego love. Never fight yourself, always embrace all parts of yourself with love—ultimately this will dissolve resistance to spiritual awakening and communication with the unseen realms.

First think of a tree that you know and love in your waking reality. The most important point to make about this tree is that it must be real, as this will help you return from your meditation 'grounded'. Be comfortable, either sitting or lying down indoors or outside, but outside would be best. Shut your eyes and, using all of your senses, find yourself standing at the foot of this tree. Look down at your feet on the ground and notice what you are wearing. Touch the trunk and notice how the bark feels beneath your fingertips. Look up into the branches above and notice what season you are in. Are you looking at soft spring blossom, lush foliage, crimson autumnal leaves or bare branches, stark against the sky? Smell the air. Is it perfumed from the first flush of blossom? Is it fresh with the scent of damp foliage or moist earth? What can you hear? Chattering birds in the tree, rustling leaves in the wind, or is all calm and still and silent?

Now invite to your inner world an animal or bird that can take you up into the sky, to your very own 'enchanted garden'. Ask if it is your guide. If it isn't, wait for another. Don't worry if it is an animal as, here in your magical world, it won't need wings to fly. This animal or bird will hold special significance for you, and after this meditation look up its symbolism. Better still, ask it why it has chosen you. What guidance has it to offer you?

Now touch your new spiritual ally and allow it to fly with you, up into the air. You could also shrink in size, or your animal could get bigger to enable you to climb upon its back. Up you go, into the sky. Higher and higher you fly until, upon looking down, the tree looks like a tiny speck beneath you. Then ask your animal/bird to take you to your very own enchanted garden—a place of rest and repose, a sanctuary where you are safe and all your needs are met. Eventually, in the distance you spot a pair of gates leading into a most wondrous garden, of which you catch just a tantalizing glimpse. You descend to the ground in front of these gates. Take time to look at these gates as they will help you to locate your enchanted garden in future visits. They could be intricately carved wooden gates, or graceful, arching silver or golden gates. They could be covered in brilliantly coloured gemstones. Let your imagination give rise to these gates. Now, push them open and enter your very own garden and refuge on the inner planes. Beckon for your animal/bird to enter with you. Know that no one can enter your garden unless you invite them to.

Now take time to explore your garden. Is it formal or informal, or perhaps a mix of both? Does it contain any trees? What plants are growing there and which flowers are in bloom? Is there a pond or stream or fountain in your garden? Are there statues, seats, or perhaps a summer house? Use all of your senses to find yourself in your enchanted garden.

Finally, when you feel you know every inch of your garden, sit or lie down in a comfortable place and call in Queen Maeve. She will present herself in a form taken from what is available in your subconscious. For me, I generally see a golden glow and feel relaxed and warm. Introduce yourself and ask for any guidance you need for your earth garden or any questions you have about faeries. Queen Maeve can also provide guidance for your personal life and she has often helped me with advice about my role as a mother.

If you do not receive the guidance there in your inner world, know that it will come to you during your normal waking state. You may overhear a conversation or open a book at the right page, or switch on the TV and catch a dialogue that perfectly answers your question. You may have a dream or just a sudden 'knowing'. We are all different and so it follows that our guidance will appear in different ways for each of us.

You can also ask Queen Maeve for healing in your earth garden, and again this may present itself in many different ways—as colour, sound, a feeling, or she may give something to you symbolically. Give yourself as much time as you need to connect with Queen Maeve, and then finish by asking her if there is anything you can do for her. Often it will be something that is environmentally focused or something that will help to inspire others. Then thank her and know that you can connect with her in your enchanted garden or in a meditative state, any time you want to.

Leave through the gates with your animal/bird and fly back down to your tree. Feel your feet on the ground, look around you to take in the familiar surroundings and then open your eyes. Take time to write down any information or impressions you receive and to fully come back to the here and now. If you need to ground yourself further, stamp on the ground and blow out sharply three times.

4. A BIT ABOUT FAERIES

There are three main types of faeries: faery elementals that help the plants to grow, faery races and faery guardians. These three types form an evolutionary ladder separate to that of humanity.

Faery guardians have chosen to help a human evolve, and in doing so mutual evolution occurs. A human can have several Nature guardians. For instance, I have a guardian gnome and a guardian water dragon. Guardians reside in seventh heaven, in 'Hollow Earth' (an energetic space within the earth).

Faery elementals that tend to an individual plant do not have free will. They can evolve and then look after a whole species of plant rather than an individual plant. They may then be called a 'deva'. These in turn can evolve into a deva of place or 'genius loci', such as a garden or a larger area, providing a template for physical form.

Faery races and faery guardians do have free will and their dominant body is emotion-based, whereas we humans are intellectually led, although this dominance is changing for both races.

All faeries vibrate at a much higher frequency than humans, and therefore are not as solid and can't be seen by the average human being. Faeries have changeable form and an individual human will 'see' the faery according to how their mind 'clothes' it.

Faeries have no need for money. I have been told this is a man-made concept invented by the 'few' who seek to have power and dominion over others. Faeries can instantly manifest what they want, but some things need group manifestation. I was shown beautiful gossamer-like silver threads, much like spiders make, that the faeries manifest to make their clothes. The word 'thistledown' came to mind.

We see ourselves as the wisdom keepers of our beloved multi-dimensional Mother Earth and we work alongside the more evolved elementals such as gnomes and dragons as well as unicorns and mermaids. We have tended the planet whilst you humans have slept. Now some of you are waking up and will work alongside us in stewardship of the earth. This will include activating codes held deep within the land at specific times, and clearing energy lines.

Faeries don't eat in the same way that we do. They take in prana/chi/ vitality directly from the plant kingdom. When humans have stumbled upon faery celebrations with great banquets, these foods are illusory and pure prana, manifested for spectacle and fun. Stories have been told where humans have eaten faery food in 'faery land' and then been unable to return to their own world. This has only happened with unfriendly faery races, and my faery guardian tells me that if one was invited to a faery celebration by friendly faeries, one could eat their food.

As faeries have no need to work for money, they have plenty of time to pursue their passions, such as the arts or healing. Any other number of subjects are pursued. They also love to have fun and they do love to dance. In fact, their whole way of life is much 'lighter' than ours and more joyous and filled with love. Some do mischief in our world but generally this is purely for fun. Occasionally a faery absorbs 'dark' human emotions and becomes 'bad' and often is cast out of the faery community to wreak havoc in ours. I am told faeries are evolving an intellect and this occasionally has led a faery astray too. My faery guardian says that if we both learn to stay heart-centred, we can't go far wrong!

It is a rare event for babies to be born, since faeries live for hundreds of years, but when they are born, they grow up much more quickly than in our world and they are brought up by a whole community, as faeries don't live in family units like we do. When a faery 'dies', they have chosen to evolve to another level.

Faeries don't need sleep like us as they have no need to process brain information like we do, but they do have periods of rest, for example when a flower faery has tended to a plant that has finished flowering and is not in active growth. When a faery rests they are assimilating experiences.

Faeries love birds and anything that flies, like dragonflies and but- terflies, and often accompany them on the wing for fun. They can also influence their behaviour to get our attention for fun or to get a message to us. One summer, whilst sitting in the garden, a butterfly kept flying around a 'Green Man' mosaic that I had made which was hanging on the fence, and then disappearing behind it for minutes at a time. This really got my attention. It then started to alight on a crystal amongst a group of crystals that was placed beside me on the ground. The butterfly continued alternating between the Green Man and this same crystal for ten minutes before flying away. At the time I was starting to explore the faery and Nature spirit realm and so I became really excited! My faery guardian says faeries can also shape-shift into butterfly, dragonfly, bee or bird form, but they would then appear more ethereal and fleeting to our eyes. I have also had an experience of this when a turquoise bird flew down in front of me whilst I was driving my car down a country lane, and then again the following day as I was entering the hospital where I worked. On both occasions the bird was there one minute and the next it was gone. This occurred at a time in my life when, unbeknownst to me, my long-term boyfriend was planning to break up with me. He ended our relationship that weekend, which was out of the blue and left me devastated and unwell for a period of time. I believe Queen Maeve was warning me that something was about to happen, as her symbol is a bird.

Animals, especially cats, can often see faeries when we can't. I was sitting in my front room one summer-solstice evening, watching a film with my family, when all of a sudden my cat stood up on my lap and stared at the doorway. I received the name Queen Titania, but as I wasn't as knowledgeable then, I turned back to the film and eventually my cat relaxed and curled back up on my lap. It was a few years later, when I was reading the book *Messages from Nature Guardians* by Fiona Murray (now known as Alphedia Arara) that I realized I had received a visit from Queen Titinius, who is in charge of the faery queens such as Queen Maeve. More recently I have reconnected to Queen Titinius and received guidance from her, which tends to focus on the bigger picture with regards to Mother Earth and our soul's purpose for being here. Faery queens are also goddesses, an aspect of the divine feminine, available to guide us as well as the faeries.

I have also had the pleasure of communing with a faery race, the magical faeries of Danaan, also known as the Sidhe. Queen Maeve has told me that there are many faery races living around the world. There were more but some have ceased to be, although they are recorded in earth history. They are much taller than faery elementals and do not have wings, although they can shape-shift and appear to us in a more recognizable form. They have a much longer lifespan than humans, and can live for hundreds of years before 'choosing' to let go of their outer garment and stepping into spirit. This is because faeries never get sick. I am told that falling sick is born out of an illusion that one is separate from the Source and therefore wholeness.

The Sidhe/magical faeries of Danaan came through a portal in a crystal I have that is from Achill, an island off the coast of Ireland.

> We live in a different dimension to physical earth. Our reality is like quicksilver, mercurial and fleeting in nature, ever forming and reforming within a blink of an eye. We create at will.

I was then taken by the hand through the portal of the crystal, but first I anchored myself to this world with a silver cord held by my power animal, Bear.

At first I saw a kaleidoscope of colours until I focused my eyes, and then images appeared of houses with tall pointed roofs. I looked away and then, when I looked back, they were gone. One of the faeries told me that my subconscious was creating these images. Then I saw a glittering sea. I was told that because I was in a magical land, images were being fired from my subconscious mind, and that I have a real love of the sea.

> We are responsible for guarding the secrets of magic, in its purest form. It is neither good nor bad but can be used for either. So, we were charged with keeping knowledge of magic safe, away from humanity when you fell from grace. Magic was known about in the times of Atlantis and used by a high priest of magic who later incarnated as Solomon. Magic was a facet of alchemy and used for creative purposes. It wasn't a separate form of energy in Lemurian

times of unity. It wasn't needed then, as everyone was connected to the Source and instantly manifested what they needed straight from the Source energy. Magic wasn't used by the general population of Atlantis but only used by high priests in positions of responsibility. They worked with the fae, harnessing the power of magic and studying it in a co-creative common goal for good. It was then misused in the era of Atlantis' long demise. Then finally we were called upon by the Galactic Council to retreat to an alternate dimension, taking magical knowledge with us, away from humanity, due to the temptations it could pose and the possible havoc it could wreak. We have guarded it under 'lock and key' ever since, and very few—in other earth dimensions—have access to it, such as Merlin, a Celtic wizard of earth magic and knowledge.

Pure magic is magnetic, alluring and disorientating, much as faery land has been described. It can confuse your mind and can tip people over the edge, especially those with mental health problems. There are dark faeries who can be summoned to your world by dark individuals, and then magic is used for bad purposes. Those with mental health problems can also be used by dark faeries, often without their consent. Eventually, magic used for dark deeds will consume the individual and arrest their spiritual growth. We are magic. It flows through our veins in its purest form, and in times gone by we have granted wishes to humans we have crossed paths with—the memories of which have been recorded in your so-called faery tales—but there was always an exchange. However, we never took a human into our reality against their will. This was made up by those who followed the Christian faith who were fearful of us, so they described life in faery land as being one of torment. Time does pass differently in faery land and so it is possible that if a human chose to return to their own dimension, then a much longer time would have passed. Our race has no quibble with humanity, and to those that call on us who have faery blood and are pure of heart, we will offer guidance and healing and co-create with them, if it is *for the highest good.** *Those of you of the faery faith can help bring back the fae into human waking consciousness in your own unique way.*

The Sidhe faery queen then appeared, her tall frame dressed in glittering white, and said:

> *Love this creation of yours [this book], and this love of the fae will flow through the pages to the readers and carry the intention with it, that they will wake up to faery existence. It will take a long time for the fae to be remembered, but in the meantime bring as much light and love into your bodies as possible. It is only by working together as a community that you can achieve the peace, love and fulfilment you so crave. You can do very little in isolation. Come out of your heads into your hearts, and love. By holding more love and light our worlds can draw nearer.*

So how does one get to meet a faery? Certainly not by chasing them! They come to you on their own terms, and this is a subject for a whole new chapter—so turn the page to find out!

---

* See chapter, 'How to connect with faeries in your garden'.

5. FEAR OF CONNECTING TO THE FAE

You may have an irrational fear of connecting to the fae—I know I did. There may be several reasons for this. Firstly, when Christianity, in its corrupt fear-based form, swept these isles, its effect was to divorce us from our true nature and Nature's kingdoms, including that of the fae races. Much later, during Victorian times and its renewed interest in the fae, much fear-based superstition was unfortunately also resurrected. We have collectively inherited this fear. Morgana Le Fae is a Celtic faery queen/goddess who can help us release our fears. She is the keeper of the land of the faeries situated under Glastonbury Tor, in an alternate dimension. She teaches us that fear arises when we disown part of ourselves and project it 'out there', where it becomes our shadow, both individually and collectively. To dissolve our fears, we have to shine the light of awareness on them. Morgana can help us to become aware of the root cause of our fear and then to integrate and heal this part of ourselves.

In heart-centred awareness/meditation, call Morgana forth and ask her to show you why you fear connecting to the fae. She may show you in pictures or you may see/hear words; you may be shown your fear in symbolic form or you may just suddenly know where your fear has arisen from. It could be from this lifetime or a past life. Once you are aware of the nature of your fear, ask Morgana to shine her healing light on it and witness this aspect of yourself healing. Once you sense that the healing is complete, thank Morgana and ask her what you can do for her, in the meditation or in normal waking reality. Morgana is an amazing spiritual ally to work with and can help you with all of your shadow work and journey to wholeness.

The next chapter explains how we can connect with faeries, but if you want to ease yourself in gradually, start by specifically calling in a flower/elemental faery and then progress to your guardian faery.

Finally, invite a connection to a member of the faery race. By connecting to an elemental faery first, you will be so delighted by their beautiful, uplifting energy, that you will become eager to progress with your connections!

6. HOW TO CONNECT WITH FAERIES
IN YOUR GARDEN

Connecting with faeries is where actions speak louder than words. If you have consciously created a wildlife garden using organic methods, and have great love for it, then the faeries will respond to your consciousness.

First, create sacred space within your garden. Designing your garden with secret areas, not immediately visible upon entering it, creates a natural setting for this. If you feel the surrounding area/garden is disharmonious, then you can place the crystal, black tourmaline along the boundaries at intervals, especially at each of the corners of your garden. Dragons can also be great allies for guarding sacred space. In meditation/heart-centred awareness, summon dragons of protection and/or your guardian dragons into your garden and ask them if they can weave protection around its periphery. They can also be asked to place protection around you as you meditate.

You can also create sacred space by invoking Nemetona, who is a goddess of the sacred grove. She is Celtic in origin and her name is derived from Nemeto, meaning a consecrated space or grove containing an altar at the centre. In heart-centred awareness, ask her to be present and create sacred space for you with the intention that the fae will feel welcome.

Connecting with faeries in the garden is made easier by creating a faery altar with the intention of creating a focal point for meditating and building up a relationship with them. They will sense this, especially if your approach is light-hearted and playful. We do need to be carrying a certain quotient of light and love and to be heart-centred to perceive them. If you are too serious, this lowers your vibration and they will have difficulty connecting with you or they might not want to be in your company.

An altar dedicated to the fae can be as simple as a rock with sacred objects upon it or a more elaborate mandala of crystals or natural objects. Let your imagination run free and create something that is beautiful and unique to you. Spirals and circles are natural Mother Earth shapes. The fae love all types of crystals, including amethyst, fluorite, rose and clear quartz. They also love anything beautiful from Mother Nature, such as pretty stones or interestingly shaped pieces of wood, flowers and shells. As the fae return to humanity's consciousness, more and more faery decorations are now available, although Queen Maeve has said that the fae prefer homemade things created with intention and dedication. However, if you do buy one, you can cleanse and dedicate it to the fae, in heartfelt ceremony. Faeries do love mirrors. My faery guardian says they are like beacons from our world to theirs. They also love silver bells and the sound they make, as well as chimes. Pretty lights around the place where you sit is a nice idea, but don't go overboard with artificial light at night. The faeries prefer natural lighting as well as natural sounds like running water.

So, once you have created a sacred space within your garden, be still, relax and focus your awareness in your heart. I usually shut my eyes at first as this helps me concentrate and stops me becoming distracted by a gardening job that catches my eye! I have found it helpful to first awaken the 'faery within' oneself before calling for faery allies. The 'faery within' is the aspect of yourself which is fae in origin; a 'second nature' self, past-life in origin, when you may have lived as a faery or were the product of a faery and human coming together. Some describe it as having faery blood. This aspect of yourself will help you connect more easily to the fae. So simply ask to connect with the 'faery within' and see or sense this aspect of yourself stepping forward.

The 'inner faery' is an actual being in another dimension. So, ask for a faery ally who wishes to connect with you, to step forward and join you, and stay alert with all of your senses. Depending on your dominant sense, you will either see them with your inner vision or, if you are clairvoyant, you may see them with your eyes open. They will take on a form depending on your subconscious. You might catch an unusual scent or sense the atmosphere around you changing—a slight breeze may start to play around you, or the temperature may alter. It is interesting to note that if your eyes have been shut, you may find—as I do—that when you open them, colours seem more vivid and the plants seem more vibrant.

Once you feel a faery is present, introduce yourself and ask their name. Ask if they are your guardian faery or an elemental faery of a flower or plant. You may be blessed with a visit from a member of a faery race, such as the magical faeries of Danaan, also known as the Sidhe. I do remember on one occasion when I was first communicating with the fae, a member of the Sidhe faery race called in but didn't say a word to me! It just watched me in curiosity and then left.

Ask them how you can make your garden more wildlife- and faery-friendly. Ask them if they have any guidance for you personally and whether you can be of service to them. Your aim is to become allies and co-create a better world for both humanity and the fae. You may not get any information the first time round, but do make sure you leave a gift on your faery altar to thank them. This can be in the form of food. They will take the energy from the food but rarely the physical form, so once an offering has been made, dispose of the food the following day and don't eat it.

There are times during the course of a year where the veils between the worlds are thinner and it becomes much easier to contact the faeries. These are the full and new moons, solstices, four Celtic fire festivals and the equinoxes.* Dusk and dawn are also magical times too.

Once you have started to commune with faeries in your garden, you may start to get unexpected or out-of-character impulses on how to garden or where to place particular plants. Follow these as they may be nudges from the faery realm, and a stronger connection will be formed if you carry out these 'ideas'.

---

* Imbolc, beginning of February depending on the moon; Spring Equinox, 21-22 March, Beltane fire festival, end of April/beginning of May, depending on the moon; Summer Solstice, 20-23 June; Lammas, beginning of August, depending on the moon; Autumn Equinox, 20-23 September; Samhain/Halloween, end of October, depending on the moon; and Winter Solstice, 20-23 December.

Finally, as mentioned before, don't forget that laughter and joy raise your vibration and make it easier for faeries to connect with you, just as being too serious lowers your vibration. Then faeries won't want to be around you, being creatures of joy themselves.

Which leads me to the next chapter...

7. FAERY'S MESSAGE OF HAVING FUN

Elemental faeries love to dance and they do so for many reasons. Firstly to raise energy, which creates a portal through which they can transport healing energy from their realm to ours for plants and the landscape. They also dance to express their delight, for they love to have fun. They laugh and make merry at the drop of a hat and can't understand why we don't take time to have more fun. They see life as glorious and one great big cause for celebration. When they create mischief in our world, it is often to provoke a reaction and to lighten us up—to help us see what is under our noses that will make us feel in awe or chuckle, depending on what it is. They also dance to raise their own energy and contact with their higher selves. They say *'Life is one great dance from season to season with none of your autumn melancholy or winter blues. Be enraptured by the natural world all year round. We are intrigued by your seriousness as we do not experience this in our world. Through mirth and making merry you will find it easier to be at one with your higher selves and so much more content.'*

8. MEDITATION TO MEET YOUR FAERY GUARDIAN AND RECEIVE YOUR FAERY NAME

Remember that imagination is the gateway to other realms!

Imagine that you're in a beautiful wood full of silver birches at springtime, the sun's rays highlighting their papery white trunks. A soft breeze causes their tiny leaves to dance and flutter and sends up the wonderful scent of bluebells and wild garlic nestled beneath them. Your feet crunch along the track as you make your way deeper into the wood.

You pass a ring of toadstools and you can feel the strong magic but intuitively know you cannot stop here.

On and on you go until the track bends sharply to the right and there, to your left, you spot a patch of foxgloves. They are unusual in that they are white, and your eye is drawn to one in particular which seems more luminous than the rest. As you gaze at this plant you feel drawn to it and you shut your eyes, giving in to this sensation.

You feel that you're gently drifting upwards in a spiral of white light, and as you reach the top you find yourself in a meadow of the most beautiful flowers you have ever seen. The sun is high in the vivid blue sky and you can hear a skylark singing, its melody so soothing to you. All the colours surrounding you seem more intense and other-worldly.

You start to walk, feeling intense love for each and every flower you see—so exquisite, so perfect. Then you begin to feel very sleepy and lie down amongst the fragrant flowers. Feeling the sun's warmth, you drift into sleep.

Suddenly you are awoken, and as you open your eyes you realize time has gone by and the sun has changed position in the sky. You hear a rustle in the tall grass, and there before you appears a being of light. As you focus your eyes, you see a face that appears human and yet is not. You know intuitively this is a faery and you feel so excited and grateful to be in its presence.

Telepathically, you feel this faery greeting you and telling you their name and you reply through your mind. This faery explains that they are your guardian faery and that they can be called upon whenever you need guidance.

You ask for guidance now, in this phase of your life. Give yourself time to receive this wisdom.

You then ask what you can do for them. It may be information for tending your garden or a patch of land near you.

They then bestow upon you your faery name which you treasure in your heart, ready to use if you have the good fortune to commune with the fae in the future.

When you have finished communing with your faery guardian you thank them and the very next second they are gone! You blink and suddenly you are standing by the foxglove patch in the woods. It is dusk and you realize much time has passed and you hurry back, feeling slightly chilly but incredibly blessed for this magical experience.

9. HOW TO CREATE A GARDEN FOR THE FAE

Everyone has a yearning to get back to Nature—to get back to their true nature. If you dedicate your garden to building a bridge between your world and the fae, then the dialogue begins!

Faeries like wild, uncultivated places where Mother Nature can carve her own design into the landscape. Here the magic is at its strongest and helps the fae create a portal from their world to ours. Certain plants like foxgloves* and heather are also notable portals. Fluidity within the garden is important, allowing Nature to self-seed, expand and move where faeries dictate. Often plants that just appear can be faeries' handiwork. Incorporating self-seeding plants contributes to a low-maintenance garden, as does keeping the soil covered by plants or mulch (a layer of loose material to retain moisture in the soil and suppress weeds, e.g. wood chip, straw, newspaper). Exposed soil is quickly infiltrated by less welcome plants and lets water run-off, encouraging erosion and nutrient deficiency. Self-seeding plants can be annuals, biennials and short-lived perennials. Some examples are *lunaria*, teasels, evening primrose, poppies, foxgloves, love-in-a-mist, *aquilegia*, *verbena bonariensis* and my favourite, the small daisy *erigeron karvinskianus*.

There are many other plants that are favoured by the fae, such as herbs with their medicinal properties: rose, lavender, clover and *artemisia*, which brings in the energy of the goddess Artemis. The fae love small bee-friendly plants. Artificially bred, neon-coloured flowers have no place in the faery garden. Native plants are ideal as they support many more insect species than non-native species, providing food for creatures further up the food chain. However, non-native plant species can also be a good food source, one example

---

* See foxglove in the section on 'Plant Spirit Wisdom'.

being buddleja from China, adored by butterflies everywhere. It's very important for your garden to provide nectar for bees over the winter and into early spring, when they are making their first forays for nectar. Plants such as pulmonaria, winter-flowering clematis and honeysuckle, native primrose—*primula vulgaris*, mahonia, winter-flowering heather and the catkins on willow, all fulfil this criteria. Also, it's important to include late autumn-flowering plants such as asters, *rudbeckia hirta*/black-eyed Susan, open-flowered dahlias and sedums. Examples of long-flowering plants and my personal favourites are perennial geraniums and penstemons. Plants that are bee-friendly and also support a more relaxed style of planting are umbellifers such as Queen Anne's lace, *knautia macedonia* and ox-eye daisies. Grasses also contribute to a more natural feel, as does the creation of transitional areas between habitats, which also serve to support a richer variety of wildlife.

Each plant has a unique spiritual energetic signature and needs to be placed thoughtfully and with respect to neighbouring plants, which is where faery guidance is extremely beneficial. Think of your garden's plants as collectively forming an orchestra—the right notes need to be grouped together to create a harmonious sound. On a physical level, this will translate into grouping plants together which need similar soil conditions and aspects of sun or shade. Gardens where plants have been placed with an ear for harmony will flourish, be pleasing to the eye and invoke a deep sense of serenity, singing to us on a soul level.

However small your garden is, a portion of it can be left to its own devices, providing food for caterpillars, such as nettle. Often the back of a garden is a good place for this, especially if neighbours have also done so. This wild area can then form a continuous corridor from garden to garden, protecting wildlife as it moves about. Creating places in your garden that are attractive to wildlife is increasingly important as intensive agriculture reduces biodiversity in the countryside.

Composting is also a great way to enrich your soil. If you grow comfrey, the leaves can be added to your compost bin to accelerate the decomposition and enrich it, and it can also be used to make liquid plant feed.*

An over-tidy garden upsets the natural balance of things. Nature exhibits an endless cycle of life and death, and as winter rolls in it is important to leave leaf litter, which will help wildlife to overwinter, and seed heads, to provide food for birds. So try and be a more relaxed gardener!

A word about furniture in your garden. Obviously, wood is favourable over plastic. Hardwood, such as oak from sustainably-managed forests, is best as it naturally lasts for decades. Timber preservatives for softer woods often contain toxic chromium and arsenic, so it is best to avoid these and choose from the ever-growing range of environmentally friendly preservatives that a quick internet search will reveal.

The fae like running water and ponds dedicated to wildlife, and if you collect rain water this gladdens their hearts. The fae love your world just as much as theirs and it saddens them to see us treating ours so badly. Foster gratitude and reverence for your garden and use it to align yourself to the sacred within. If you garden with love, your garden will reflect this back to you and the fae will be better able to connect with you. Indeed your garden reflects your emotional state of mind. Your garden reflects back to you your state of consciousness, so where there are problems look for the corresponding issue within. For example, weeds (wrong plant, wrong place, and highly subjective!) can symbolize the negative thoughts, attitudes and beliefs or unprocessed emotions that you need to address. Of course, the symbolism expressed in your garden will be unique to you and only you can interpret it. Gardening consciously in this way is another approach to healing. The plants you are drawn to—your favourites—are the plants you need for your journey back to wholeness, and if you take time to sit in your garden with the intention of receiving healing, then you will. Better still, meditate with your favourite plants.

When gardening the faery way, try to link with every plant. Plants respond to love and appreciation, helping them to flourish. Faery

---

* Comfrey for gardeners can be found, for example, at: www.gardenorganic.org.uk

elementals help plants to grow by pouring their love and blessings onto them constantly. All things respond to love and will grow. In fact, there will be a two-way blossoming! Say hello and bless the plant and then ask it if it needs anything from you. To receive answers you need to rest in your heart-space. Here is a method for taking your awareness into your heart-space:

Take a seat in your garden and close your eyes; breathe slowly and deeply, relaxing your body. Take your awareness to the soles of your feet and imagine roots growing from them, down into the ground beneath you. Imagine the roots growing to the very centre of the earth and wrapping around a crystal. This is the heart of Mother Earth. Rest there a while. Then take your awareness back up your roots, through the soles of your feet, up your spine and then out through the top of your head, all the way up to the sun and the Source/Father Sky. There is no right way of doing this—just intend it and it shall be so. Rest here a while. Now that you are connected to Mother Earth and Father Sky, take your awareness into your heart-space. To help you do this, focus on your breathing and the rise and fall of your chest. Then imagine that you shrink in size and intend to step into your sacred or higher heart. Once inside, take time to look around you. It could look like a room, a cave or a chapel. It will be completely unique to you. It will feel very peaceful here and your mind will no longer have a hold on you with its distracting chatter. Take time to look around you and then rest here a while. Now open your eyes and visit the plant you intend to commune with and, with your new heart-centred awareness, greet it and ask what it needs from you. Take the first thought that comes into your awareness. For example, it might need watering or a feed, it might need mulching or it may even be asked to be moved. With practice, you can learn to shift into heart-centred awareness in the blink of an eye. It will depend on your emotional or mental state or how busy you were prior to entering the garden.

Even before entering the garden set the intention: *what do I need to be aware of, what needs my attention?* Connect to the spirit of your garden or genius loci (see Chapter 10).

A word about slugs and snails attacking your favourite plants. If a garden is overly cultivated, there may be an unnatural concentration of plants which are irresistible to these creatures and therefore the population will increase, sometimes to epidemic proportions. This would not occur in the wild and is a consequence of the artificial situation you have created, especially if you have lots of container-grown plants, providing shelter for slugs and snails. The faeries have told me that even using organic slug pellets alters the balance in the garden and that—if you love the collection of plants you have—the best solution is to invite the next predator up the food chain into the garden, e.g. hedgehogs and birds, by creating the right conditions for them. So, for birds introduce a bird-feeding table or plants with berries. For hedgehogs leave areas wild for insects to flourish in, to provide food as well as a place to hibernate in. You can also programme a quartz crystal to strengthen a plant (see Chapter 11) or use nematodes (slug parasite). You can also, in meditation, talk to the oversoul (non-physical counterpart of a species) of birds/hedgehogs and invite them into your garden.

When gardening, there are two ways to approach any given task. One way is to 'do to', where we are mostly in our heads, not paying much attention to what we are doing and more focused on our mind chatter. The second way to approach a task is to 'be with', where our awareness rests in our heart, listening to guidance from our intuition/soul on how to carry out the task—and even whether the task needs carrying out in the first place.* If we are totally absorbed in the task at hand, this then becomes a form of meditation. See your approach to your garden as a metaphor for how you approach life. Do you approach gardening by striving and toiling and never enjoying? Use your garden to cultivate a right relationship to the land, the wider world and to yourself. Approaching a given task in the garden, one can take it to different levels of awareness. For example, let us suppose you have decided to prune the rose bush. First, become heart-centred and 'be with' the task of pruning, really noticing the beauty of the plant and taking great care

* See Michael J. Roads, *Conscious Gardening*.

with each cut, coming into harmony with the rose. This is a form of meditation, whereby the only thing that exists for you in each given moment is the rose and the action of pruning. Taking your awareness to a deeper level allows you to commune with the spirit of the rose/ deva and its faery. The deva* of the rose carries the blueprint of what that rose will look like in optimum vibrancy and health, and information can be sought from the deva as to what that rose needs. If one sees the deva in meditation, it will be specific to that person; the mind of the gardener will 'clothe' the deva to assist in communication and this image could be very different to another person's experience. However, seeing is not essential for communication. The faery elemental carries out the instructions for the deva associated with that rose and can give information on what the rose needs for optimum health. One can also ask to receive wisdom/guidance from the deva of the rose for your personal healing. Gardening then takes on a whole new meaning of co-creativity, which was how it was in Lemurian times. The more you interact with your garden, the more it interacts with you!

* Deva is the Sanskrit word for 'being of light'.

10. SPIRIT OF PLACE / GENIUS LOCI / DEVA

Every garden will have a spirit or deva that looks after it and orchestrates all the individual Nature spirits found within it. Sit in your garden and take your awareness to your heart-space, then ask to meet with the deva of your garden. You might see a colour or feel an energy. You can even ask for a name. Then ask what you can do to help it create a garden that will encourage and support wildlife, Nature spirits and faeries, and will be a sanctuary for you.

The deva of my garden introduced himself as Paulo, which means place of rest. In reality, I feel that devas are neither male nor female. The deva of my garden conveys to me information in the form of knowing and feeling rather than words. Unlike the Nature spirits and faeries, Paulo also conveys only a few pieces of information at a time, whereas I find faeries are much more 'chatty'. In my first encounter with Paulo, he conveyed to me that my pond is a vital part of the garden's ecosystem and that I needed to eliminate its blanket weed in an organic Nature-friendly way. I only have a very small pond and it was getting smothered. He encouraged me to link with the spirit of the pond to get further information. At first I was guided to make a gem-elixir by placing the crystal aquamarine in a bowl of water and leaving it in the sunshine for a few hours, then pouring this energized water into the pond. This revitalized the water but didn't eliminate pond weed, and so I did some research and found a product that used a bacteria that eliminated blanket weed but was safe for all the wildlife in the pond. This did the trick. I then placed a small, tumbled piece of aquamarine into the pond to ensure the ongoing vitality of its water.

Subsequent communications with Paulo revealed the bigger picture of my garden. Again, through knowing and feeling, he showed me that the area alongside the kitchen of my L-shaped house was very important in relation to the energy of the house and the garden. He showed me that the energy of our neighbour's ash tree was very important to my wellbeing and encompassed my garden. Paulo showed me that flowing love to my garden allowed it to reciprocate by flourishing. He conveyed to me that my relationship to my garden can be seen as a metaphor for my life. By holding love in my heart for all things, including friends and family and extending this to the world, puts me in the right relationship to everything. As a consequence, love flows back to me. All things grow in a response to love. Paulo showed me another metaphor; that if I strive and toil in my garden and never stop to 'smell the roses', this can mirror how I approach life as a whole. The result would be to always feel discontented and low in vitality. So, the garden can be used as a practice for right living.

I was shown the garden as sacred (as all land is) just by virtue of it having sprung from Nature, and told that it should be treated as such. If I maintained a state of reverence and gratitude towards it, then this would align me to the sacred or Spirit. He then showed me that, as deva of the garden, he was the microcosm within the macrocosm. Thus, he related to the deva of the surrounding area, who then related to the deva of Worcester—and on it goes, in larger and larger magnitude, a natural harmony of co-creativity. He conveyed this to me in the form of a small circle within a larger circle, which in turn is within a larger circle still, and so on.

11. THE USE OF CRYSTALS IN THE GARDEN

There are many types of crystals that can be used in the garden to help plants to flourish and to attract the Nature spirits and the fae. Here are some of my favourites:

Serpentine

Serpentine to me is a crystalline form of Nature's green ray. When you hold it or meditate with it, it will help you connect to the natural world. When placed upon the ground, its energy 'snakes' through the land, freeing up any stagnant energy and making it available to the Nature spirits and elementals to help them carry out their individual functions within the garden. It also initiates a rising to the surface of Gaia's creative impulses, awakening the higher intelligence of Mother Earth. Gaia is the soul of Mother Earth and its male aspect is Geb.

In practical terms, one would see a greater vibrancy and vitality within one's garden. When held, (preferably one in each hand and one placed at the sacrum), serpentine can also facilitate an awakening of one's kundalini energy, a maternal spiritual energy which lies in a dormant state, coiled up in the sacrum bone. Once awakened, this can lead to a state of 'self-realization' or enlightenment—where the human spirit becomes one with the divine, and fear and anger are replaced with joy and inner peace.

The darker version of serpentine, that also contains magnetite, works more with the magnetic grid of the earth, strengthening it. In turn, the vitality of plants is protected and is less affected by extraneous influences. Faeries and Nature spirits are better able to retain their integrity and fulfil their roles more efficiently. The pale version of serpentine is more attractive to faeries. Constructing a mandala of serpentine and other crystals such as clear quartz or moonstone, with the intention of supporting faeries and Nature spirits in their work, ensuring optimal growth of the plants, will work wonders in the garden. Alternatively, find the heart of your garden and place a clockwise spiral of serpentine to facilitate the upward free-flowing of energy throughout your garden. The genius loci of my garden, Paulo, showed me where the heart of my garden was and conveyed that if I set up a seating area as near to this as possible, this would help me to feel heart-centred and serene. One clue as to where the heart of your garden is would be its proximity to the head plant* which orchestrates all of the individual plant energies. The heart of the garden isn't always in the centre!

Infinite crystal

There is another form of serpentine originating in South Africa which is more grey/green and is called the Infinite stone. The energy of this type of serpentine feels more subtle and rarefied and helps you connect to that still point within your heart. It can be placed on the ground where you like to sit in the garden to help you feel at one with Nature. This feeling is enhanced if it's placed in the centre of an infinity symbol made out of quartz points, with the first loop on the right following a clockwise direction and the second loop on the left of the Infinite stone pointing anti-clockwise. To radiate this energy out to your garden (otherwise it would keep travelling around the loops) place three quartz points above and below the Infinite crystal in the centre, pointing outwards.

Healerite

I feel healerite is gifted from Mother Earth specifically to help at this stage of our evolution. It's from north-western USA and is a bright lime-green. It works with the green ray of Nature and the Christ Consciousness grid to restore the latter in areas of deep destruction such as bomb sites. In our own gardens, where there may not be any areas of destruction, healerite can nevertheless strengthen the Christ Consciousness grid. This is both a blueprint and template for earth and is both holographic and fractal in nature. It is based on a stellated dodecahedron. It distributes the life-force energy and provides templates for material creation. I see healerite in meditation as a pulsating golden light. This crystal also provides excellent healing

---

* 'Head plant' is explained in the chapter, 'Plant Spirit Wisdom'—Rose.

for us too, working on all levels of our being, from the heart and solar-plexus chakra and auric field, to our cells and organs.

Seriphos

Seriphos is a form of green quartz found exclusively on the tiny Greek island of Seriphos in the Aegean Sea. The leaf-green colour of the blade-shaped crystals comes from the mineral hedenbergite. When I connect to this crystal, I see a god of Nature called Seriphos who looks like a cross between a Greek god and the Green Man! He told me, '*Mother Earth gifts seriphos to those who have an ear. My crystal represents an intermediary stage between the plant and crystal kingdom. It will enhance your ability to hear messages from plant spirits and in turn will help the plant spirits to hear you better. You can connect to me to receive my wisdom on anything pertaining to planet earth.*' He then told me that unity consciousness would soon be birthed on our planet.

Green Kyanite

The crystal green kyanite builds a bridge between our consciousness and Nature's unseen realms, facilitating a deeper appreciation and understanding of all the forces at play in our garden. Connect with this crystal in heart-centred awareness/meditation and then place your awareness in each part of the garden and ask to be shown anything which needs attention. I was shown a narrow area outside the dining-room window where the energy was stagnant and so I placed a solar fountain there to circulate the energy. I was also shown that the heart of my garden needed marking/honouring. So I created a circle of rose quartz crystals there. Also, the elementals and Nature spirits weren't best pleased with my tiny circle of artificial turf in front of the pond (too small for real grass) and showed me a spiral stone mosaic, or a lawn of chamomile which does not require mowing, that would be better.

Malachite

Malachite is another beneficial crystal for the garden. I was guided to place this in the area of the garden that had stagnant energy as it radiates harmonious energy, facilitating a rushing-in of Nature spirits to help with raising the vitality of the area.

Structures can also be built to channel cosmic energy into the land in order to strengthen the flow of energy through the earth and shift any blocks. You can intend to activate and strengthen the elemental grid. Supporting and strengthening elemental activity will bring more balance and harmony to your garden and an abundance of vital, healthier plants, and this in turn will give you an increased sense of well-being. You could in fact hold any number of positive ideas close to your heart, such as awakening compassion in the world. I asked my guide Taliesin to show me the best way of doing this during a shamanic journey, and he took me to the underworld and showed me a reindeer. Puzzled, I didn't immediately see a connection until he pointed out a cairn of stones with two antlers placed on the top, forming a funnel or 'v'-shape. He explained that our ancestors built structures like this to channel cosmic energy into the land as well as inviting gods and goddesses to be present when conducting ceremonies.

We can recreate this in our gardens by finding a 'y'-shaped branch from a tree of our choosing and placing the point where the 'v' meets into the ground. Ask the deva of your garden or the gnomes to show you the best place to pierce the ground in order to channel the light of the cosmos into the bones of Mother Earth. I was shown that this structure needed to be placed in front of my pond, which I was told already channelled in cosmic energy, but that this process would be enhanced by the structure. I was also shown how to lay out an anti-clockwise spiral to channel energy to the centre, using stones, crystals or flowers petals, although the latter obviously will not be as permanent. Remember that your intention is key to activating the energetic purpose of this structure, without which it will just be a twig in the ground. If you wish, you can call in your guides, the fae and even Mother Earth herself to help with your sacred intention of activating this cosmic channelling.

Clear, Amethyst and Rose Quartz

These can be programmed to support the flourishing of plants in our gardens. In heart-centred awareness, hold the quartz in your hand or place it at your heart chakra or third-eye chakra (sits between your brows). First, ask whether the crystal is happy to be programmed for this function. If it is, then state your request in a clear, concise and sincere manner. As long as your words are heartfelt, then the crystal will align to this intention. For example, if a plant is not growing very well, you can say: 'For the highest good I ask that you now attune to this plant, bringing it much light and love to ensure its health and vitality, and so it is.'

Once you have placed your chosen crystals on the ground, sit by them in meditation/heart-centred awareness, with the intention to activate them, feeling their energy and receiving further guidance about them and whether they need tweaking in any way. For example, I was told the antlered serpentine structure would channel in different cosmic energies, according to the needs of the land. It is always good to request a spiritual ally, such as Queen Maeve or the genius loci of your garden, to oversee the work of the structure. I added the quartz points at the centre of the infinity structure when I realized in meditation that the energy was just circling round and round. You may receive guidance to place specific crystals in certain areas of your garden. In meditation I was guided to place a rose quartz in a specific location of my garden. When I asked why, I was shown that I still harboured grief over the loss of a tree next door, close to my fence. It had been beautiful, with amazing spring blossom and gorgeous blazing leaves in autumn, but because the neighbour felt its roots were disrupting his garage floor at the bottom of the garden, he had it chopped down. The love radiating from the rose quartz was love towards the tree, now in etheric form, and healing for my sorrow in losing it. Again, this was placed with the intention of performing this work.

The earth, and all life upon her, is in the process of rising in vibration from a third-dimensional frequency of duality consciousness, to a fifth-dimensional frequency of unity consciousness. Crystals are gifts from our Great Mother to help with this transition, for our own enlightenment and for creating our sacred gardens.

12. THE ANCIENT CIVILIZATION OF LEMURIA AND OUR GARDENS

As our earth and all of the kingdoms upon her ascend, including humanity, we are being brought closer to the energies of Lemuria, an ancient civilization pre-dating Atlantis. I feel that if we can anchor Lemurian light energy into our gardens, then we can help with Mother Earth's evolution, creating a place of love and peace that can radiate out to the surrounding land, facilitating the embodiment of more light, much like the ripple effect in a pond. The fae and Nature spirits will adore our gardens and our plants will flourish. We will feel amazing too!

Lemuria was a time of unity consciousness; everyone was of one heart. Each individual was unique with skills specific to them, but they knew what the others were thinking and feeling and adjusted what they were doing accordingly, in order to work as a cohesive whole— much like bees in a hive with a common goal, a 'hive consciousness'. Lemurians co-existed and co-created with angels, the fae races, the Elven Ones, Star Elders, Nature spirits and elemental faeries, unicorns, mermaids, dragons, dolphins, to name but a few.

Gardens were sacred public spaces, woven from trees and plants, flowers and crystals and metals, specifically tellurium. This is a shiny silvery-white semi-metal that has a brittle crystalline form and today is found in combination with other metals such as gold. It is extremely rare but more common within the cosmos. In those times, the Lemurians knew how to obtain it and work with it, form- ing astonishing sculptures within their gardens. (It is mildly toxic, so presumably the Lemurians were immune or knew how to make it safe.) All of the precious metals were used in garden statues and buildings as the currency in Lemurian times was love. These were the original gardens of Eden, which King Nebuchadnezzar II tried to mimic in his famous Babylonian gardens—a faint echo of the memory of the Lemurian gardens. These were places of sanctuary where the Lemurians visited for healing and to be re-balanced. Due to the unity consciousness, collectively the Lemurians would be aware when an individual needed aligning/healing and the individual would take themselves off to visit these healing gardens. This was seen as a sacred duty, performed for the benefit of the whole. These gardens were open day and night and visited in quietness, much like a library today. Upon entering, the individual was drawn intuitively to a specific area of the garden, to a specific plant or crystal or to the raised pools of mineral-rich healing water. The over-lighting deva of each sacred garden, together with the 'god of Nature',* would assess what the individual needed and then these energies would be generated by the garden's plants, Nature spirits and crystals. These energies were wrapped around the individual like a cloak of light, which became one with them. The Lemurians also visited these garden in pairs recreationally, again in quietness, which wasn't difficult as they communicated telepathically.

So how do we make our very own Lemurian Garden of Eden?

We can recreate a healing garden for ourselves by using plants that we are drawn to. Generally, these would be the ones we need energetically. Plants already growing within our garden may also be the very ones we need. As our health is a dynamic state and requires different things at different times, so too are the plants that we need, changing from season to season, year to year. The use of crystals and ponds with fountains will also generate a beautiful energy, as mentioned in previous chapters.

You may also be lucky enough to have a Lemurian seed crystal. Lemurian seed crystals are quartz that has been coded with sacred

---

* When I connect to these gardens, I am shown the Greek god Dionysus. He is the earliest representative of the power of Nature, or Green Man, that has been recorded in the form of a leaf-clad statue found in Naples in Italy and has been dated at 420 BCE. I feel his later representations and qualities have strayed from his original, pure nature.

knowledge in Lemurian times. So far, three types have been found—clear, golden and pink. If you are the guardian of one, it will be because it holds wisdom for you to access and for you to share with the world in your own unique way. They can also be placed directly into the garden, acting as antennae attracting high-frequency light into the land. To find out where best to place them, become heart-centred and see where your intuition tells you, or ask the genius loci of your garden or the gnomes who work with the land (see the relevant chapters).

Finally, in heart-centred awareness, ask Queen Maeve or your faery guardian what else you can do, specific to your garden. For example, I was shown individual plant energies as ribbons of light, flowing and weaving together. However, these energies were finding it hard to cross the patio in the centre of the garden. I was then shown how to create a goddess spiral counter-clockwise, in moonstone, serpentine and malachite crystals (first asking their permission). This would act as a focal point, bringing the collective energy of the plants together into the centre of the patio.

A guided meditation to visit a garden in Lemuria for healing

Not all of us 'see' when we meditate. Trust your senses or knowing. The healing still happens!

Shut your eyes and take your awareness into your heart-space. To help you focus here, breathe in and out of your heart, making your out-breath longer in order to relax. Once you feel relaxed, intend to enter your sacred heart, an energetic dimension within your heart chakra. Imagine a rainbow bridge forming there with the intention that it will take you to a Lemurian garden for healing. Step onto the rainbow bridge and cross over. There, in front of you, are incredibly ornate silver-coloured gates, made of tellurium. As you approach them, they swing open. You are expected! Step inside. Use all of your senses to find yourself in this garden. Touch the bark of a tree, a velvet petal of a flower, crumble the soil beneath you… Look up in to the sky—is it day or night? Can you feel a breeze or the sun on your skin? Smell the air. Which scent is being carried on the wind? Can you hear birdsong? Look around you at all of the plants and trees. Take your time to really find yourself here.

You see a figure approaching and recognize Dionysus in his purest, high-vibrational form, known to us as the Green Man. He is dressed in green robes and in his hand he carries a pine-cone staff. He has long golden curls and his head is adorned with a circle of leaves. He leads you to a clearing and on the floor you see a huge twelve-pointed star mosaic made of tiny red, black and gold tiles. Dionysus motions you to stand in the middle of this star. You feel the genius loci of this garden appearing around you, and Dionysus explains that you are being assessed for the type of healing you require. Then Dionysus leads you to an area of the garden that you need. Pay special attention to the type of plants in this area and see which ones you are drawn to. Sit with them a while, perhaps holding part of the plant in your hand—a leaf or flower that you take with permission. Invite the spirit of the plant to be with you and give you healing. Again, use all of your senses in order to make the imagination of holding the plant in your hand as real as possible. Really look at it in fine detail and feel its texture and smell its scent. Remember, imagination is the gateway to you experiencing this dimension/timeline. Or, you may have been led to one of the raised pools which you get into, relaxing in the mineral-rich warm water. You may also be visited by a Nature spirit, the fae or Elven One,* a gnome or unicorn… Allow yourself to be surprised by who turns up and greet them, full of gratitude for the healing they offer and any wisdom they impart.

Sit here in these healing energies for as long as you need, and when you are ready call Dionysus, who will take you back to the gates. Thank

---

* An Elven One is a term taken from Elen Tompkins book *Silver Wheel*. From my understanding, they are the original creator angels (Elohim) and came to earth in Lemurian times. They are reaching out to us at this time to help with the ascension process.

him and then cross the rainbow bridge, returning to your sacred heart. Give yourself plenty of time to gently come back to waking reality, and integrate the healing energies you have received.

13. THE GREEN RAY OF NATURE

This is what Queen Maeve told me about 'the green ray of Nature'.

The green ray of Nature is generated by the Green Lady and the Green Man, the former being an aspect of the goddess/Mother Nature and the latter being the male form. The green ray of Nature is everywhere. It is in and of all things in the natural kingdom. It causes every single leaf and blade of grass to grow and as such is also called 'the ray of abundance'. Queen Maeve says that in the world of faeries they are all naturally attuned to the green ray, and it is partly how they create things, together with a ray which we would call 'magic'. The green ray is rising in frequency with Gaia.

Queen Maeve says that in the future we will perceive tangible differences when out in Nature. Plants and trees will seem more vibrant with colours radiating in intensity and it will be easier to see the energy behind form, the Nature spirits and faeries. This level is already in existence for those who are 'seers' and carry more light. To attune to this higher frequency of the green ray, it is as simple as asking the Green Lady and the Green Man for this to happen. Do this whilst sitting in your garden with your eyes shut. Be centred in your heart, receiving in love and gratitude. This is enhanced if you place your bare feet on the ground. Then open your eyes and look around you in reverence and see how your perception will have altered. You will also feel very peaceful and centred. Once attuned, you can flow this green ray down from your crown chakra at the top of your head, to your heart and then down your arms and out of your hands. You can use this energy when gardening. See how it alters your perception of what and how you do things in the garden. This will become automatic over time and is an explanation of our term 'green fingered', where plants flourish under your care, and it will be easier to see Nature spirits and faeries—if they want to be seen!

More recently, the crystalline emerald ray, which is a higher vibration of the green ray, has been returned to our planet. The emerald ray awakens the emerald codes within our DNA, and as a result a higher state of consciousness unfolds, which allows us to access wisdom on how to take better care of our beautiful planet and find heartfelt solutions to the environmental problems humanity has created.*

* More details on the emerald ray can be found on Alphedia Arara's website elementalbeings.co.uk

14. QUEEN MAEVE'S SEASONAL MESSAGES

Queen Maeve has taught me that it is very important to be in tune with the seasons and to respond accordingly. This will ensure we stay in better health. Gardens are never static and they change, not only from season to season but also from moment to moment. We can use our observations of our gardens to connect with the seasonal changes within us.

Queen Maeve's message in the season of winter
Just as the bare bones of the earth are revealed, so are we stripped bare as we enter this time of introspection. If we tune into the season and to ourselves we can respond accordingly, and if we can't respond immediately then we need to ringfence some time later. In the silence of being, thoughts and feelings will surface, to be addressed and laid to rest. Now is the time to ponder what we have achieved this year and where we are heading. What are our dreams?

Without dreams we are adrift at sea, being pulled this way and that by other people's expectations and desires. It is always best to go with the flow but to still have our dreams to navigate by. Now is the time for getting more sleep, nurturing ourselves by the fire, to cosset, nourish and dream; taking long leisurely baths with essential oils, wearing soft, warm natural fibres, and tuning into what nourishment our bodies need. But there is a balance in all things and too much sitting by the fire will leave us sluggish, both physically and mentally. Taking long walks in Nature and really noticing our surroundings and any messages that come our way with the animals, birds and plants we meet,* will reinvigorate us. Remember, what we resist persists and so it is easier to wrap up warm and embrace the cold and the wet, rejoicing in the season of winter, rather than to shun it and moan about the weather.

---

* Avia Venefica's website whats-your-sign.com is helpful in guiding us to understand the message an animal or bird may be bringing us.

Do not tidy up your garden too much before winter truly sets in. Plant and leaf litter can provide a home for a host of beneficial creatures overwintering, such as hedgehogs and ladybirds.

Queen Maeve's message in the season of spring

Spring is a time for dancing your dance and singing your song that is authentic to you. It is time to unleash your creativity and to bring into manifestation the dreams you nurtured during the winter months. Don't forget that the most fulfilling creative projects will be born out of love and soul expression, not fear and ego. Choose one or two that seem most exciting to you and formulate an action plan as to how you will achieve them. If you do not have a vision for the coming year, then spend time outdoors just *being*, and see what inspiration arises that needs expression—then have the confidence and trust in yourself that you can make it happen and go for it!

Spring is also a time for honouring our sexuality. As the sap is rising so too are our sexual desires. Do not make the mistake of separating your sexuality from your spirituality. You are an expression of the divine, and expressing our sexuality is a sacred part of ourselves.

Finally, spring is a time to rejoice in all of the good things in your life. Rejoice in the new growth you see all around you and the new growth within your life too.

Queen Maeve's message in the season of summer

Sense the energy of fullness, ripeness and oneness of being at the pinnacle of vitality. High summer is just that! It makes us feel high! It is intoxicating, heady and holds us in a warm embrace, where we can feel at one with ourselves and all of Nature. If we flow with the energies of summer, we will feel at our most creative within our chosen field. We can feel relaxed and yet inspired, content and adventurous. We are full of vitality, love and wonder for all of Nature's creations—a veritable feast of colour, scent and the sun's warm embrace on our skin—our hearts open, centred in love, where we can open our spiritual eyes most easily and see into the metaphysical dimension of Nature. Indeed, at the solstice, when the veils between the worlds are at their most thin, we can step into other realities easily and effortlessly. There we can see the fae celebrating, dancing and making merry, spiralling upwards in pure love and joy—spreading their magic over the land as it crackles with vitality and vibrancy. Rejoice as the fae do. You are pure love, pure joy.

Queen Maeve's message in the season of autumn

Autumn's energy is one of ripeness, fullness and abundance. Luxuriate in the last of the summer sun, storing it in your brow chakra for the long winter months ahead. Autumn is about paring down all of your duties and chores to the bare necessities. Life is now about gathering in your energy. Turn inwards to see what nourishment you need, gathering all of your experiences, successes and failures and turning them to your own stories in order to nourish your inner landscape throughout the winter months and to generate new ideas for the springtime.

15. WEATHER

I spoke with Queen Maeve and asked for a definition of 'weather'. She gave me a visual picture of an ever-evolving mandala of earth, air, fire and water elementals, and said:

> *Weather is the end product of a dynamic process of Gaia seeking balance and stability for all of her kingdoms. Many moons ago, in Atlantean times, there was an attempt to control weather with the use of giant programmed crystals, but this ended in cataclysm. In ancient matriarchal times, weather was seen as a sacred expression of Mother Earth/goddess. Only with patriarchal distortion and separation from the Source, did sacrifice in times of drought occur, of both animal and human, to appease the gods as humanity sought to manipulate and conquer Nature. In truth, see weather as a glorious expression of Gaia, the most sacred of planets, and when extreme weather patterns occur, look closer at the impact humanity's activities are having on the planet. It is so peculiar that you would want only blue sky and sunshine and that your mood is so dependent on it. Why, nothing would live without rain!*

Then I spoke with the Magical Fae of Danaan:

> *Ah yes—weather! It causes much mayhem in your world—much worry and stress. We are bewildered by it—truly we are! There is a higher intelligence to weather patterns. Weather is a response to planetary impulses and Gaia's shifts in consciousness, as well as being affected by humanity's collective consciousness. Weather patterns are nothing more than the cycle of life made manifest—an ebb and flow, cyclical in nature. Add to this the environmental chaos you humans wreak and Gaia's ascension process, and you have a veritable mix of phenomena. Thousands of elementals are at play (including many you have no name for) in manifesting weather. It is a very intricate process.*

Then the dragons of weather stepped forward. They felt extremely powerful:

> *We are the dragons of global weather and have a key role to play in manifesting weather patterns. We 'seed' global weather patterns at the instruction of Gaia (Mother Earth's soul) and this then evolves through numerous other dragons and elementals, influencing local weather patterns. This is a beautiful, harmonious and synergistic dance responding to Gaia's call of that which is needed to sustain harmony and balance in her many kingdoms. However, as Gaia's inner 'merkabah'* has recently turned (January 2018) and at previous times in history—this has an added impact on weather patterns. As Gaia ascends, she has need to shed lower energies, that are not in alignment with the evolution of light, upon and within her kingdoms, often resulting in earthquakes. Sadly, from a limited perspective these cause loss of life, although always in divine accord and soul contract.*

As mentioned previously, weather patterns are also affected by humanity's impact on the environment, such as loss of trees and rising carbon dioxide levels, depleting the ozone layer (recently there have been reports that this process is stabilizing). As I understand it, if humanity treats Nature's kingdoms with more respect, and if we align ourselves harmoniously with Nature, then weather systems would flow more smoothly.

It is also important to change our response to 'weather'. Firstly, ignore the news (unless a tornado is on its way!) which largely reports our weather patterns gilded with doom and gloom warnings—weather apps are often wrong. We can gauge when to garden just by opening our senses and looking up into the sky! Love all weather patterns and marvel at the tremendous interplay 'behind the scenes' that is bringing you each weather condition. Weather engages all of your senses. Marvel not only at the beauty of sunshine but also the wildness of

---

* This is a light-body based on sacred geometry, existing simultaneously in all dimensions of time and space.

wind and the revitalizing effect of rain, or be exhilarated by thunder and lightning. It is a way of feeling truly alive and can be invigorating, if you intend it to be so. Just dress accordingly. Be grateful we are on such a glorious planet! Blue sky is uplifting, but we can intend to store it at our brow chakra to sustain us through the darkest of winters, as can conscious connection to Gaia's inner sun—her heart. Cloud formations can inform you, if you intend guidance to present itself in this way. As mentioned before, Nature acts as our mirror.

There are also gods and goddesses, that are found in myth and legend all over the world, who can influence weather if they are called upon, but always for the highest good. Thor is a Norse storm god and Zeus is a Greek god of thunder and lightning. One can call upon their energy during a thunderstorm, harnessing this energy to increase the potency of manifesting—always for the highest good for all concerned. Other examples are the Slavic goddess Perperuna, goddess of rain. She can be called upon to cleanse anything we no longer need in our life, and the African Oya, Yoruban goddess of winds, tempests and cyclones, who can also be called upon to help us embrace change.

So what can we do to assist Gaia and influence the smooth unfolding of weather patterns? Firstly and most obviously, we can reduce our carbon footprint on the earth. Walk or cycle; reuse and recycle; eat local and organic where possible; turn off lights etc. when not in use and support clean energy sources such as wind power; install solar panels; reduce consumption of water. These are just a few ideas. On top of this, rejoice in all weather conditions. Know that if enough people feel sad, gloomy and fearful, there will be grey skies—and conversely, if enough people's hearts are filled with love and joy, then clearer skies ensue, but always in alignment with the bigger picture.

Ask Gaia in heartfelt awareness/meditation if she needs help with regards to nurturing any of her kingdoms during extreme weather conditions. Obvious examples are feeding birds in winter and making shelters for hedgehogs, ladybirds and bees; constructing log piles for toads and frogs and not clearing up our garden in winter so that it is neither sterile nor without shelter. In times of little rain create a pond or a birdbath and shaded areas and don't plant new plants unless you are prepared to water them regularly.

We can also link with the dragons of weather in heartfelt awareness/meditation and ask for specific elements such as rain in times of drought—but first check that this is for the highest good for all concerned, as we ourselves are not privy to the whole picture.

I have a sense that global warming will continue but will eventually stabilize as we change our habits, but that in thousands of years' time there will be a final Ice Age.

But we must concentrate on the *now* and our soul's contract for being here.

16. GARDENING BY THE MOON

Queen Maeve speaks:

The fae live and garden by the moon cycles—therein lies health and harmony. When the moon is waxing, culminating in the full moon, we recommend that you plant, as the life-force is rising. This is the time to create things of beauty and passion in your life. When the moon is waning, the life-force is flowing inwards and the fae do not plant and create new things.* Pruning can be done now. However, we would continue to tend that which we have initiated in the waxing phase.

A new moon is the time to rest and replenish, to hold gratitude and love in your heart, flowing it out to your garden and yourself, friends and family... It is a time to dream new ideas, to set new intentions.

A full moon is time for celebration, to dance and make merry; to give thanks for life and love! It is also a time for letting go of any discord in your garden. Dig up that which is no longer serving the greater whole. This applies to you too! Let go of all that no longer serves you. Write it on a piece of paper and burn or bury it.

You will also find that by following the moon cycles, pests and diseases in your garden will lessen, and within yourself your health and well-being will be stronger. 'Moon time' is the only clock the fae have. They know that time is an illusion—a man-made way of organizing life to suit a logical, linear mind. But the fae know that all time is now. In this given moment, deep within your sacred heart, you know what needs attending to. You know if you need to rest, to move, to eat, to sleep, to meditate, to create, to spend time with a loved one, to cherish a child...

---

* Root crops should be planted in the third week of the waning moon cycle.

The same goes for your garden. Sit in it, go into your heart-space and ask for what needs your attention right now in this time of the waxing or waning moon and listen/know the answer in your heart. It's as simple as that. You have a tendency to over-complicate things. It is in your very nature—although this is changing as you come home to yourselves.

When you live by the moon, as opposed to man-made time, you will feel there is a time for everything and everything has a time! As a consequence, you will feel more peaceful and content, more rested and, ironically, you will be more productive! This is in stark contrast to always feeling that you are chasing your tail; that there is not enough time, and feeling tired and below par in health.

Let the moon be your ally!

17. DRAGONS

There are many types of dragons. Those found on the earth are light conceived by Mother Earth's soul, such as elemental dragons of the earth, sea and sky and fire dragons of the volcanoes. There are also rainbow dragons, ice and snow dragons and white, fire dragons of ascension in Earth's inner planes, as well as dragons of the cosmos—galactic, intergalactic and universal, to name just a few! We may also have guardian dragons who can work with us, providing healing and guidance in our lives. All have specific roles to play in the unfolding of 'the Plan'—the ascension of Mother Earth and all upon her—and as such are vital and integral stewards to Mother Earth's health and evolution.

Many moons ago, dragons of the land lived upon the earth in physical form and we sought their wisdom and healing. When Christianity flooded the land in its bastardized form, divorcing us from our true nature and Nature, these earth dragons became a foe to be sought out and slain—a symbol of humanity conquering its own inner nature and Nature. Humanity turned against itself, giving full power and authority to the Church for divine communion with the god/dess and in doing so, we cut ourselves off from our inner divinity as well as plundering the land for its resources.

Earth dragons have become the stuff of myths and legends, portrayed as the enemy, taking treasure and doing battle with humanity. (Dragons have long been associated with guarding treasure such as gold and jewels. These treasures symbolize light codes that have been locked away, ready to be activated according to divine timing.) In reality, dragons were only ever our allies, but once we turned against them, they retreated into Hollow Earth (a term for a holographic and multi-dimensional space within physical earth). There they have waited until humanity gained sufficient enlightenment, awakening to its true nature. They now ask us to embrace them once again and co-create a heaven on earth—and to teach our children about them too.

There are many types of dragons that you can get to know within a garden setting, such as dragons of the elements—earth, air, fire or water. They will have much wisdom to share with you, and healing for your garden and for yourself. Sit in your garden in heart-centred awareness and call in a dragon, holding the intention that this particular dragon can help you garden with more awareness of Nature's hidden realms—the elementals and the fae. An example of an invocation might be: 'I call forth from the dragon realms, in love and in light, a dragon to assist me in taking care of my garden, to help me garden with more enlightenment, nurturing the Nature spirits, elementals and the fae, in order to increase the vibrancy and vitality of my plants and creating a sense of well-being and healing for all those who spend time here. Namaste.' Then sit in silence, using all of your senses to detect when a dragon connects with you, whether it be through sensations, words, images or just an inner knowing. Introduce yourself and ask for the dragon's name. Ask if any area of your garden needs healing and if so, how you can facilitate that with regards to specific plants or crystals, or whether the dragon can do the healing for you. Just as you have meridians within your energetic body, earth dragons keep the equivalent open and flowing in Mother Earth's body.*

Always give thanks after receiving dragon wisdom and leave a gift in your garden of something shiny. They especially love gold!

Another way to work with dragons is via a crystal dragon skull. In more recent times, they have become available in crystal shops. Dragon crystal skulls act as physical reminders that dragons exist and are ready to work with us to co-create a better world to live in. If you decide to buy one, activate them by holding their third eye—usually a horn is carved here—to your third eye and welcome them in to the crystal. Then hold them in the palm of your hand and, in heart-centred awareness, link with them and sit in their energy, getting to know them. You can ask them questions to find out how you can work together,

* For further explanation of how dragons heal the land, see Chapter 21 on Gnomes.

not only in your garden but also globally. In October 2017 a dragon portal opened up on earth and new dragons came through into the inner earth cities to help with raising the consciousness of the planet and all of the kingdoms on and within her.*

---

* Further information on dragons can be found on Alphedia Arara's excellent websites www.elemental beings.com and Dragonwisdomschool.org

18. ARCHANGEL PURLIMIEK—ANGEL OF NATURE

When I first linked with archangel Purlimiek, I cried! He had such a beautiful energy and it felt like coming home. His colour is a gorgeous blend of blue and green. He told me that a great way to connect with angels in Nature is through cloud gazing! He says that to watch the cloud shapes form and reform as they pass by alters your state of consciousness, and if you intend to connect with an angel of Nature the cloud often takes on the shape of an angel!

Nature is in every one of you. It is a calling to be at one with yourself. It is a coming home to yourself—that still centre within. Nature brings you into alignment with your soul, which then nourishes you at a very deep level.

I orchestrate devas of Nature, who are closer to the vibration of earth; who in turn orchestrate Nature spirits and faeries, who are closer still, to create the seasonal stimulus for plant growth—and a loving, nurturing energy. When tapped into, this energy allows you to slip into a state of being. Nature exists as an intricately woven web of co-creative beings, from goddesses to faeries, to gnomes and dragons—all fulfilling their roles together, never in isolation. Nature is a pure state of 'being-ness' and potential for creativity. It holds space for and allows the creative impulse to manifest. Another name for Nature is the Green Lady or the goddess, and nothing can come into being without her involvement.

My message to humanity is to learn from Nature. Look to cooperate with each other, working towards a common goal of love, peace and harmony. This involves truly listening to each other and to Nature herself. Being in Nature more will be healing and will naturally put you in touch with your truth. You will feel better for this and more inclined to work for the common good. Individually, collectively and planetarily, the importance of this cannot be overlooked. It is fundamental for the survival of your species. A minimum of an hour a day spent in Nature, whether it is in your garden, park or the countryside, will transform the way you feel, think and ultimately act.

It was fast approaching the spring equinox when I connected with archangel Purlimiek, and the birds were very active and singing like there was no tomorrow. I realized that birds and animals and the insects all respond to the calls of Nature in the springtime without question. They can't be any other way. It's only us who don't respond, because we have divorced ourselves from Nature's seasonal energies and thus are out of alignment with our true nature/soul. This can then manifest within us as 'dis-ease', and collectively in society as war and conflict.

Too much emphasis has been placed by humanity on 'doing' and on the intellect and not on 'being' and 'feeling'. Your ego then runs the show and the soul's impulses are forgotten.

By connecting to Nature regularly, this imbalance can be corrected and will result in a permanent change in how an individual or society will want to live their lives, operating from their heart and guided by their soul. The more people who prioritize spending time in Nature, then the greater change you will see in your society. It all starts with you!

19. MASTER PAN

I contacted Master Pan as a ninth-dimensional master of light. He told me he communicates with different factions of humanity in various guises and varying vibrational rates such as the Green Man and Cernunnos. I asked Master Pan for a pictorial representation of who he is, and I received an image of a beautifully complex green fractal/mandala. I sensed that within Master Pan are all of the dimensions of Nature from the third dimension upwards, and some still as pure potential. I asked Master Pan to bless and strengthen the Elemental grid* I had activated in the garden, which he did. He said:

> There are many more elementals than you currently know consciously. The faery-race kingdoms overlap with your realm and that is why you have been aware of them, although for many of you this has now passed into myth and folklore, as the fae chose to withdraw in order to survive the harsh environment you created. The faery-race realms know that earth is ascending, just as you do. Many of them are curious to see if humanity re-remembers the fae from this higher state of awareness. I am talking of the faery races, not your flower faeries, as you have named them, for these are air and fire elementals. The faery races applied to come to earth just as you did, and various animals, crystals and plants, although some of these originated here on earth. I hold these many different kingdoms of Nature together, in potential harmony, although humanity has chosen to develop their intellect out of all proportion to their emotional and spiritual nature. This has resulted in human beings over-identifying with their mind and ego, resulting in their disconnection from their true nature and their place in Nature. This has been allowed due to your having free will and so we all watched to

---

* The Elemental grid is the matrix that holds the elemental energy on the planet. For further information see www.elementalbeings.co.uk/nature-spirit-and-earth-healing-retreat-scarborough-2016/

see what would happen, sending various help from time to time over the course of your history. In Atlantis and Lemurian times, the faery races walked with humanity and hybrids were created by some of you, as you joined your light bodies together. This has proved to be important now, in that those of you who have faery 'blood'/light codes, once activated (by simply asking), can reawaken to the truth that faery races exist and build bridges between humanity and the fae.

I have been demonized by your world religions, depicting me with horns (forgotten antennae to the Source/god/dess) alluding to my having a beast-like nature, as humanity sought to rise above Nature, not realizing that this cannot be achieved since you are Nature and the so-called 'beast' is your raw, inherent, instinctual nature. I am pure love from the Source just as you are, and my role is very simple: to hold the template of all of Nature, including humanity, to the highest level of light that can be achieved. At a certain percentage of light, dense physical bodies cannot exist and are discarded for light bodies. This is the same for all—the fae, animals, crystals, plants as well as humanity. Go into your heart-space and invite me in and I will inspire you in whichever way is appropriate, in order to reawaken you to Nature and your role within it. This I pledge to you.

20. QUEEN TITINIUS

This communication occurred on the Celtic festival of Beltane on 1 May, when the veils between the worlds are thin and contact with faeries is easier. Queen Titinius, who oversees all of the faery queens, had tried to contact me a few years previously, as mentioned in a previous chapter. It was the evening of the summer solstice and I was sitting on my sofa cuddled up with my family watching a film. All of a sudden our cat Maya sat up and stared at the doorway. The name Queen Titinius came into my mind and I knew she was a faery queen, but this was before I was consciously trying to communicate with the Nature realm. I felt torn between going outside into the garden and seeing if I could receive a message whilst continuing to watch the film with my family. The latter won but our cat continued to stare for what seemed like ages.

So on this occasion, at Beltane, I was sitting in my greenhouse, heart-centred, waiting to see who would talk to me at this auspicious time. I felt Queen Titinius step forward. She has a very strong energy and I saw dark pink and red. I wondered if this was her signature colour and she answered by saying her colours/energy change, depending on the season and how active she is.

> I reside over all of the Nature goddesses. Nature is an intricately detailed tapestry of complex energies and I oversee each of these threads. My role now is also to awaken humanity to the importance of co-creation with Nature's energies on our beautiful planet. I am specific to the British Isles but there are others like me in other countries. The balance of Nature and its harmony depend on good stewardship and responsibility by humanity. Humanity is not part of Nature, humanity is Nature—one thread in this intricate tapestry and there is a need for balance with the other threads and not to hold dominion over them. But human beings often fail abysmally with this, due to being disconnected from their true inner nature/divine gifts.

So, I repeat, you are Nature, and so cannot exist outside of it with-out upsetting your inner balance of body, mind and spirit and the outer balance of the world. Take time to reconnect with Nature and, in so doing, become one with your own true nature and see your life blossom with good health, great love and joy and a realization of your true purpose here. Sit in your gardens, become heart-centred and call in the green ray of Nature. Intend healing in body, mind and soul. This is as simple as it needs to be—just do it regularly. The faery kingdoms grow ever nearer to you as you hold more light. They are making their presence felt more and more, especially with those that are more spiritually aware, and yet many still regard the fae as nothing more than pure myth. Those of you that carry faery blood can ask me or Queen Maeve to activate this part of you and this then brings codes within you into being and acts like a key; a key to build bridges between yourselves, humanity and the fae, ben-efiting Mother Nature as we teach you of your role within Nature. The fae are beings placed on earth with love and intention by the Source, evolving just as humanity is. Some fae races are very wary of humanity as they cannot comprehend what you are doing to this planet. It is insanity in their eyes and it will impact them too if the earth is desecrated and the delicate balance of Nature upset. This is why they have withdrawn from your physical world and from human consciousness—many in anger as they are predominantly emotion based. So those of you who are awake, reach out your hand to the fae with the intention of learning from them—learning about Nature and the role you must play.

At this point I became aware of many bright-green elemental faeries, about a foot in height with wings like that of a lacewing (insect). They were busying around the garden inspecting everything and peering in at me in the greenhouse. Queen Titinius had called them, and they called themselves the emerald faeries. They could feel the Elemental grid and showed great interest in this. They said they would love to work with me but that in order for them to know I had heard/seen them, could I make a faery offering of honey in my best bowl! They then said that they were a facet of the green ray of Nature and looked after a portion of it. They also told me they loved the pond and the gooseberry bush, and that if I flowed the green ray of Nature through me, then it would be easier to connect with them.

Queen Titinius finished by saying, 'Love thy neighbour'. I had been harbouring negative thoughts about one of my neighbours who puts his TV on really loud, so word-for-word it could be heard in my garden. His dog often barked periodically throughout the day and the evening which really irritated me too, as I am a lover of peace and quiet. Her words were heeded, though as I realized this neighbour mirrored things in me which I didn't like about myself, as well as unfinished business between myself and my father, whom my neighbour reminded me of—so I resolved to flow the ho'oponopono prayer fo this situation. Ho'oponopono is an ancient transformational and healing technique originating in Hawaii and roughly translates as, 'to make right'. It consists of four simple sentences in the form of a mantra: 'I'm sorry. Please forgive me. I love you. Thank you.' When repeated with heartfelt intention, flowing it to the person and/or situation, the negative emotional baggage is cleared in our subconscious. Since our outer reality is a mirror of our inner reality, the problem is then resolved. As a result, we are also more deeply connected to the Source/god/dess.

21. GNOMES

I have a wonderful guardian gnome whom I call Geb. He is a male gnome and linked with the masculine energy of Gaia. There are female gnomes too, who are linked with the feminine aspect of Gaia. Geb has shown me how important it is to work with the gnomes found in your garden. They hold the history of the land and they 'lock up' negative energy. Geb has told me that in times past there were plenty of dragons that then transformed this 'locked up' negative energy into benign energy. I'm told it's an easier process for the dragons to deal with 'locked up' energy that the gnomes have processed, rather than free-flowing negative energy in the land, but in more recent times there have been fewer earth dragons to perform this function because of our fall from grace and the dense energy that then resided on the earth's surface. So, they retreated to the core of the earth but now, as Gaia is ascending, they are once more moving to the surface to perform this vital function. You can imagine how useful this function is in war-torn areas, but I am told that as 'earth keepers'—we can all be earth keepers, protecting the land from overdevelopment and preserving harmony and balance—we can aid this important process where the negative energy is too overwhelming for the gnomes to deal with. We can help through the simple process of loving the land. This in itself attracts more gnomes, dragons and other Nature spirits to our garden to deal with negative energy, ensuring the health of our land. Love is the ultimate transformational process. We don't need to understand the process; as soon as our mind becomes involved, we lose that magical connection to Nature and Nature's processes. So, focus on love for your garden and an intention to clear the land of all negativity, and then trust and surrender to Nature's process involving those wonderful gnomes, dragons and other Nature spirits. Remember that imagination is the gateway to other realms. You can do this for any piece of land. Send love with the intention of clearing negative energy and trust that this will be so.

Gnomes also anchor all of the positive energy generated over time and weave it into the very fabric of the land. I was shown golden threads and a combing action, and this process felt very fluid. Where there are breaks in this free-flowing energy, gnomes join these threads up again with the help of the dragons. This free-flowing energy in the land is essential to the health of the land. I was also shown by Geb that gnomes gather and maintain earth memory at certain energy points called 'nodes'. We can access this memory with a little practice. In my mind's eye, I see earth memory in the form of treasure chests! It was wonderful to find out that my garden and the surrounding area had been a Druid meeting place. It does feel very magical here.

So, for everything you do in the garden, ask the gnomes for their help, especially when you are creating crystal or flower mandalas and anchoring energy into the land. They will tell you where to position these and where to position plants for their optimal health too.

Geb tells me there are also specific gnomes that tend to the crystals found in the earth. On one occasion, whilst sitting and meditating in my garden, Geb told me he had brought white sapphires into the garden, in energetic form, as this was an energy that I needed. I think, perhaps, that only guardian gnomes perform this function, since gnomes of the land would be more focused on the land itself, rather than the gardener.

I have also been shown, on another occasion, a huge etheric diamond that gnomes attend to in the centre of Hollow Earth. The gnomes are wizard-like in appearance and very tall. I was shown them drawing the energy of the diamond up to the earth's surface, which then met the cosmic diamond light radiating down on us from Source. As above, so below.

PART TWO:
PLANT SPIRIT WISDOM

'The Spirit of Lavender' by Eleanor Gray

INTRODUCTION

The plant and tree kingdom can support us and help us to evolve spiritually, as can all of Nature. We just need to take the time *to be*, to connect from our heart and receive this wisdom—whether it be in the form of knowledge or healing. All of us can do this. It may take practice, but all of us can drop into our heart-space and 'feel' energetically the plant or tree before us. Another way to connect to the spirit of a plant is to imbibe it. This can be done for those herbs that you can make a tea from. Check that it is safe to do so first, of course.* Do not censor anything that comes to you—images, words, an aroma, a colour, a feeling. This type of communication cannot be rationalized, analyzed, scrutinized. It simply *is*. It is your truth, your unique message and healing, perfectly tailored for you at that precise moment in time and therefore only meaningful to you. Even if you do not understand its meaning at the time, just accept this gift and thank the plant or tree. One thing is for sure, you will never look at that particular plant or tree in the same way again!

As a gardener, heartfelt communication can only enhance the way you tend to a plant or tree. The messages and healing we receive from the plant and tree kingdom will vary from season to season and depending on our state of wholeness/health. It is lovely to have a notebook specifically to write down these experiences. Your higher self will see this as a commitment from you to become aware of the spirit, and your ability to receive information in this way will evolve as you engage your sixth sense. The message or healing may come from the spirit of the individual plant, from the over-soul of the plant species, from a Nature spirit or faery tending to the plant, or even from a facet of the goddess connected to that particular species. An example of the latter is when I connected to the plant artemisia in my garden and found the goddess Artemis speaking to me. This message came through very

---

* See for example www.herbalremediesadvice.org

easily as it was a new moon, which is this particular goddess's potent time. New moons and full moons are potent times for communicating with spirit as are sabbats—solar celebrations marking transitions between seasons—but any time is okay too. The very act of communicating in this way will allow us to step out of our busy lives and come into a more harmonious and balanced, heartfelt state of being. The more we practise, the more it will become second nature. I feel the goal is for this state of being to be our default state, where we are more fully connected to our soul—but not, as it is for most of us, to be in our head, thinking and worrying, influenced by our (lower) ego. The most important thing is to have fun with this. The more we lighten up, the easier it is for Nature spirits, the fae and plant or tree spirits to communicate with us, as we become more expansive and light-filled. Excessive seriousness lowers our vibration and we energetically contract so that light cannot flow in and be held as easily. Over the next few pages I offer messages that I have received from various plants and trees over time, including some meditations to help you connect—although, as previously mentioned, your messages will be unique to you.

Aconitum (Monkshood, Hecateis or Wagon of Venus) ~ integration of shadow-selves

I am that which resides in your deepest darkest depths of your psyche, that calls to you to be rescued, embraced, loved and healed and released into the light of your conscious awareness. My 'medicine' is for healing shadow-selves leading to your greater wholeness; revealing inner 'truths' currently playing out in your subconscious that may not necessarily be for your highest good.

Inner truths are core beliefs programmed into your subconscious from a very early age but operating in present time.

Connect with monkshood in heart-centered awareness/meditation/journeying, and ask:

'Show me my shadow-selves, those that I need to embrace and those that I need to heal/change.'

Not all shadow-selves are detrimental to living our life authentically—only those core beliefs which have been programmed into our subconscious which are 'false truths' taken on from our parents, teachers etc. and which impact on our present life in a negative, limiting way.

Then ask the monkshood to show you how your life would appear without the negative shadow-self playing out, and the first step towards achieving this.

I am finding that the most powerful method to integrate a shadow-self is by sending this part of ourselves unconditional love regularly, until we see an outward change in our lives.

In mythology it is said that monkshood or aconitum was found growing near Mount Akonitos in Pontus in Asia Minor and that it grew from the spittle of Cerberus, the three-headed hound of Hades, god of the underworld. Medea, a Scythian sorceress, was said to have attempted to poison Theseus with a cup of wine laced with aconitum. In Greek mythology the goddess Hecate invented aconite which Athena used to transform Arachne into a spider. Aconitum is sacred to Thor, god of thunder and Shiva, a god in Hindu religion. Aconitum is ruled by the planet Saturn.

All parts of this plant are poisonous. Gloves are recommended when handling it.

Amaryllis Belladonna ~ dance of life

We invite you to connect with our medicine and enter the 'dance of life/light'. All of life is made up of dancing particles of light, constantly moving spirals of consciousness. You can choose to dance in harmony with the divine or to dance out of step—the choice is yours. To dance in harmony with the spirit/goddess is to flow with her and be guided by her. To dance out of step is to choose to be guided by your ego, which creates difficulty. Then, everything will feel like an uphill struggle.

Ash Tree ~ potential & passion

Let me show you the potential that lies hidden within your depths for manifesting your truth. Let me ignite the passion to bring this potential forth into the world, as loving service to the divine. Blessed be.

I am the Sun's dance on water
I am the waters' depth of possibilities
I am the connection between the two.

I am the trident of a sea god
I am the wand of a magician
I am the shamanic staff connecting the other worlds.

I am the waters of emotions
I am the flow of life
I am the primordial mother from whom all life sprang.

To know me is to be at the centre of the universe
The still point within your sacred heart
A powerful place of possibilities.

Ash trees are male, female or hermaphrodite.

A magical way to connect to the spirit of the ash is to immerse yourself in water on a sunny day, connecting to the dance of the sun on the water whilst holding an ash tree seed/key or leaf.

Alternatively, here is a journey to connect with the spirit of the ash:

Close your eyes and start to breathe slowly and deeply, using your breath to help you relax. Focus on your toes, your feet and ankles and relax them. Relax your calves, your thighs and hips and pelvic area. Relax the whole of your abdomen, your stomach and chest. Let this wave of relaxation move up into your shoulders and spill down your arms, relaxing your wrists, your hands and your fingers. Relax your neck, your throat, your jaw, your cheekbones. Relax all of the tiny muscles around your eyes, your forehead and your mouth. Sink deeper and deeper into relaxation, focusing on your breath to carry you deeper and deeper and become more and more relaxed.

Use all of your senses to find yourself by an ash tree, one you know or one conjured up from your imagination. See your feet standing on the soil. Reach out and touch the bark. How does it feel under your fingertips? Look up into the branches of this ash tree. The leaves are just starting to unfurl and there are bunches of seeds just beneath each set of leaves. Peering through the branches, look at the sky beyond. And now with your hand still placed upon the ash tree's trunk, take your attention to your heart. Breathing in and out of your heart, with all of your attention within your heart chakra and in heart-centred awareness, call forth the spirit of the ash, making a heart-to-heart connection. Looking up into the branches, you see that the bunches of seeds are now glowing. One in particular catches your eye. Raise your arm and cup your hand and watch as this seed detaches itself from the rest and floats down into your palm. And before your eyes, the ash seed transforms itself into a glowing key. This key represents the wisdom you need at this time. A door appears in the trunk of the ash tree. Use your key to unlock this door and enter into the trunk.

You find yourself on a spiral staircase that stretches off into both directions. You are drawn either to go down the spiral staircase or up it: down into the roots or up into the branches; down into Mother Earth or up into the heavens, the cosmos. Take the steps now, winding round and round, up or down, until you take the last step and emerge into a landscape.

Look around you now, taking in all that you see. Then ask the spirit of the ash to connect with you, in the highest form that is right for you now. Merge with the spirit of the ash and receive wisdom and healing in the form of words, images, sounds or colour.

The ash gives you a gift. If it is symbolic, ask for its meaning. Ask the ash what gift it needs in return, whether in this inner world or action in your outer world.

Thank the spirit of the ash and step back into the trunk, back along the spiral staircase, back through the door in the trunk. Lock this door with your key and know that whenever you need further wisdom or healing, you can use this key to connect again.

Slowly bringing your awareness back into the room, feeling your feet on the floor, gently open your eyes.

Autumn Flowering Crocus ~ light bearer

Our medicine is to remind you that you are a light bearer—that each of you bears a chalice for the divine to fill up. It is our fondest wish that you hear the clarion call to spread this love and light to others and, one by one, that this love and light spreads across humanity until you beat as one heart, move with a common purpose, to birth the New Earth into a golden dawn of brilliance. Connect with our beauty and receive our medicine.

Bluebell (English) ~ sing your note

The words 'magical' and 'enchanted' come to mind when one steps into a bluebell wood. Bluebells 'capture our heart', and you just can't help but smile. In fact, the spirit of the bluebell, with its heavenly blue colour, can help lift depression, literally lifting the 'blues'. So, when walking in a bluebell wood hold this intention in your heart and the healing becomes more potent. The bluebells' ruling planet is Mercury and some serve as portals to the faery realm, just as foxgloves do. I am told that those of us who have the 'key' and possess faery sight know which bluebell is a portal by its magnetic pull—but always step through with a faery guide, otherwise you can become disorientated.

Bluebells also helps us to 'sing our note', which is so important at this time. Our note is unique to us and when all of our notes combine, the harmony we bring to this planet is unimaginably beautiful and uplifting. Our note can be found using this visualization given to me by a magical faery of Danaan. Remember, imagination is the gateway to other realms:

Imagine that you are walking in a heavenly bluebell wood. Use all of your senses to find yourself there. As you are walking along, you are drawn to one bluebell plant which seems to be glowing. In particular, one bell on the stem is brighter than the rest. Intuitively you know that this particular bell holds your note. Magically, you shrink to the size of a bee and enter this flower. In your heart-space, 'hear' this note. If you are clairaudient you may actually hear your note. Alternatively, feel the note with your whole body. Either way, intend it to align you to your true purpose for being here. You may 'see' images as you feel this note or be given a symbol which you can meditate with in the future and obtain further information that will help you know yourself better. Once you feel you have embodied your signature note, step out of the bluebell and return to your normal size. Give thanks to the spirit of the bluebell and return to your normal waking state. Whenever you feel out of alignment, maybe from being too busy, come back home to yourself by becoming heart-centred and imagining yourself back in your bluebell flower, feeling your note.

Broom ~ purification

Mine is fire magic—crackling intention. I sweep away all that is of vile intent.

Purification of the highest order is my magic. Mine is the alchemy of fire. Use me to purify your aura and home, restoring its sanctity.

The fae initially taught humanity how to use broom and indeed all herbs. I love the smell of broom when it is burnt. It smells to me of magic and ritual. Burn a pinch of the herb on a charcoal disc and then waft it with a feather around each room and into each corner and crevice, as well as through your aura. Remember to hold the intention of purification as you do this. I was also shown that you can sprinkle this herb along your doorstep if you feel the need for added protection. But please do not use broom out of fear. It is only natural that we sometimes pick up negative energies from time to time, and by negative I mean not in alignment with our highest good/truth. So, it makes sense to regularly clean energetically. I was also shown that we can ask the spirit of the broom to clean specific things such as negative thought-forms that can attach to our aura and home—and the charged atmosphere that occurs after an emotional release. We can also ask/intend the spirit of the broom to clear anything at a spiritual level that prevents you from aligning to your truth and authenticity, and also to clear away anything that blocks your 'sight'/intuition. We can also ask it to clear away anything that gets in our way to grounding in Mother Earth's love. I asked the spirit of the broom if it could even clear away anything preventing me from connecting to the goddess/god/All That Is. I saw an 'ascended' version step in and she started to work in my heart chakra, clearing away feelings of unworthiness. Of course, we are all connected to Source all of the time—it's just that our perception of this gets distorted.

In summary, there seems to be two versions of the spirit of the broom: a more 'earthy' version, very connected to ritual magic, and an ascended version that feels freer in the sense that it is not bound to protocol. The latter appeared to me as a tall white lady with flow-ing robes, which she used to sweep away negative energy by twirling in circles, and I saw the former as a besom (a broom) with crackling fire-red twigs and also as a rod of red fire which turned to white as she worked. Do not ask for too many things all at once if you are working on yourself because, as with all things, there needs to be a focused intent on your part, as well as time for the energy to settle afterwards.

Burdock—Arctium Lappa ~ tenacity

I offer you the gift of tenacity. Hold fast to your dreams. Focus on what you wish to manifest and let nothing sway you. Each of you has placed within your heart a sacred calling and, however insignificant you feel it to be, each one of you has an important part to play in the unfolding of earth's history at this time. Cradle and nurture your dream as you would a baby and prioritize it in your life. Dedicate each day to the unfolding of your dream. If others try to sway you, realize they are projecting their fears onto you and at a deeper level—mirroring your fears of not being good enough. You are all 'enough'!

We are here to collectively birth this new enlightened world. Every one of us has this divine responsibility. If like me you have several projects on the go, go into your heart-space and sense which you feel most excited about and is most urgent. If you don't know what your sacred calling is, again go into your heart-space where all of the answers lie and ask to be shown by your angels/higher self/god/dess (whichever term feels right for you).

I had never really seen burdock before but it was interesting to see the correlation between its message and its form. The prickly seed-heads of these plants (burrs) hook into the fur of animals and our clothing and get dispersed far and wide—a metaphor for our heartfelt dreams once manifested, rippling out to the wider community. In 1948, a Swiss inventor called George de Mestral was fascinated by the seeds/burrs that had attached themselves to his dog's fur and his clothing whilst on a walk. He studied them under a microscope and the result was Velcro!

Burdock also has an incredibly long taproot, creating a firm foundation to support its height of up to three metres. Again, this is a metaphor for how important our foundations are when pursuing our dreams: looking after our physical body with the correct nutrition, hydration, exercise, meditation and sleep; also, honouring our emotions, positive thinking and affirmations and spending time with loved ones, friends and family, and finally, grounding ourselves into Mother Earth and grounding our dreams into reality.

And, it has heart-shaped lower leaves! How amazing is that?

Buttercup Spirit Wisdom ~ the playful inner child

A golden chalice of sunshine
A bridge to your inner child
and her unquestionable connection to the divine.

Do I love butter?!
Skin reflecting gold
I can't help but smile.

Why so serious? Never underestimate the importance of play—doing something for the sheer delight it brings you! To play is to be light and carefree. It lifts your spirits and helps you to rediscover a love for life. It is important to balance your 'work' with play, and some of you have manifested 'work' as your play, which is meant to be. Connect with me in meditation and ask the highest form of my spirit to step forward and show you what stands in the way of freeing your inner child. Let me show you this in the form of an image, a word or a feeling. Then, intend to release it into the light of the god/dess. See the brightest white light dissolving your blockage to playfulness. Then ask your inner child to show you what form of play would be the most freeing/healing for them. Carry this out. This is very important! (I was shown to blow soap bubbles in the sunshine!) Regularly connect with your inner child and ask how they are feeling and what they need. Don't make this a chore. It only takes a few minutes. My golden light acts on your solar-plexus chakra and the realm of your feelings, which are so important to honour.

Cyclamen Hederifolium ~ cycle of life

Dance with me into the centre of the spiral and there, deep within your psyche, see the crone holding the maiden's hand. For inner work still needs to be done in this season of winter, so spend time in stillness and silence. As you shed outmoded beliefs, habits and all that is born of fear, new ideas will appear as tiny seeds of light within this dark cosmic womb. Come springtime, I will lead you spiralling back out, ready to embrace the goddess as maiden, pregnant with possibilities, inspiring the landscape and your life. Blessed be.

Cyclamen is ruled by the planet Venus, the element of water, and feels very feminine. I also connected with cyclamen in the season of autumn. Here is a very different message:

We herald the completion of a seasonal cycle that culminates at Samhain/Halloween, the Celtic New Year, and our message to you is the importance of storing nourishment for the coming winter, just as we do, within our bulbs.

What type of nourishment do you need that will carry you through the winter; that makes you feel good and at one with the world? Nourishment can take many forms—taking a walk in Nature and storing the last of the sunshine at your brow; eating the last of the sun-ripened tomatoes (with plenty of olive oil and sea salt!)—or perhaps creating time to 'be' within each day; maybe to include a regular spiritual practice you have been putting off?

Whatever form this nourishment takes, know that it contributes to your growing self-love, the foundation and bedrock of your being.

Dandelion ~ shine your light

Soon after I started sipping my tea made of dried organic dandelion leaves, I started smiling! I felt like I was drinking a cup of sunshine! Do you remember blowing dandelion clocks to tell the time? Do you remember blowing the dandelion seeds and making a wish?

I also remember, when we were children, if someone picked a dandelion flower everyone shouted out that the unfortunate victim would wet the bed, which caused much hilarity and probably alluded to one of its medicinal properties of being a diuretic.

I asked the spirit of the dandelion in its highest form to step forward and share its wisdom.

Shine your light and keep smiling, no matter what is happening in the world. In order to do this you need to be deeply rooted in Mother Earth's love and love for self. This will help you to feel safe enough to shine/express your authentic true nature.

It is interesting to note that the emotions that are associated with feeling happy are involuntary and are controlled by the autonomic nervous system. We cannot force ourselves to be happy, but if we smile (a true smile is where the eyes narrow slightly and crow's feet appear and the upper half of the cheeks rise) we can bypass the autonomic nervous system and signal to the brain to feel happiness—and we do! We can also use the genuine smile to trigger a smile in others. How fabulous is that!

Elder ~ she who 'brings together'

The elder has a rich history. I see her as golden pulsating light and feel her as a 'fire of countless summers'.

> My history is interwoven with yours as my bounty has nourished you on all levels. Those that know, bring their concerns to me, seeking my advice. The fae pay their respects to me as an elder of their community. I am called the Elder Mother—Queen of the Herbs.

I asked Queen Maeve of the fae to elaborate on the faeries' connection to the elder. She responded:

> We adore the elder. We too are nourished by the flowers and the berries and often our faery paths cross the elder. These are our resting places along our journey where we make merry. Deep rivers of wisdom run through the elder. It has long been told that she will be the meeting point for humankind and the fae, helping to bring us together once more. The elder is where we can all sit in a circle and learn about each other. The fae wish to teach humankind how to look after the planet from their perspective and to teach us about Nature (that which is inherent within) and our duty and place within it.

I then called in the magical faeries of Danaan and asked them to tell me about the elder.

> She is the shining one. The one who connects to all nations/tribes and the fae races and their star origins. She is the holding point and has the potential to weave us all together again—to start the lines of communication once more between us all. At the downfall of Atlantis, when the twelve tribes went forth, elder was given this gift to hold the threads of each tribe/nation of humankind and of the fae races, knowing

at some future point we would merge again as one heart—in love and unity consciousness. At the most basic level, her bounty of flowers and berries have served as the vehicle for bringing people and the fae to her; and to those that knew, she bestowed her wisdom through the ages.

I asked the elder for one last message.

There are those of you (both human and fae) who wish to stop this process of coming together, of uniting in one love. Pay no attention. Turn from them and focus on the light and on love. Lay down your differences. See yourself as unique pieces of a jigsaw that makes no higher sense until you have come together. In the completion of it, the higher meaning of life—of consciousness—makes itself known. Blessed be.

Journey to meet the spirit of the elder

We will use the following visualization technique with subsequent journeys to meet spirits of plants and trees:

Close your eyes and start to breathe slowly and deeply, using your breath to relax. Focus on your toes, feet and ankles and relax them. Relax your calves, thighs and hips and pelvic area. Relax the whole of your abdomen, your stomach and chest. Let this wave of relaxation move up into your shoulders and spill down your arms, relaxing your wrists, hands and fingers. Relax your neck, throat, jaw and cheekbones. Relax all of the tiny muscles around your eyes, your forehead and mouth. Sink deeper and deeper into relaxation, focusing on your breath to carry you deeper and deeper, becoming more and more relaxed...

I am going to count down from ten to one now and, at the count of one, I want you to find yourself by a tree that you know—a tree with happy memories, where you feel safe and peaceful. Ten, sinking deeper and deeper; nine, becoming more and more relaxed...

And one: you find yourself by a tree. Use all of your senses to find yourself there. See your feet on the ground at its roots and notice what you are wearing on them. Reach out and touch the bark. How does it feel under your fingertips? Is it rough, smooth, damp, dry? Look up into the tree.

Which season are you in? Are there tiny buds forming, or does delicate blossom adorn the branches? Maybe it is in full leaf? Or perhaps it is autumn and the leaves have taken on the colours of burnished copper and buttery gold? Or winter has stripped these leaves and the bare branches are starkly outlined against the sky?

Smell the air. Can you detect the delicate perfume from the blossom? The smell of damp soil? The distinctive woody smell of a bonfire nearby? Is there a gentle breeze or is it wild and windy?

Using all of your senses, find yourself here in the 'otherworld'.

Call in an animal guide to join you on your journey. Allow yourself to be surprised at what shows up. This animal or bird will hold special significance for you at this time; ask it what this is. You can call in any other guides and angels you wish to help you on your journey.

Now start your journey—whether walking by your animal guide, or riding on its back or maybe flying with it.

Soon you find yourself on an ancient trackway lined either side by a dense tall hedge of spindle, holly, guelder rose and hawthorn. This trackway has an otherworldly feel. The hedge is teeming with life, home to myriad forms both physical and energetic—such as nature spirits, gnomes and flower faeries. As you walk along with your animal ally, you feel the magic of this leafy green track and you sense that it has been in use for hundreds of years as a processional faery way. Hear the birdsong, listen to the bees humming, the rustle of leaves. This is a spirit road. A faery path. The trackway curves to the left and then you see, a little way before you, an elder tree making up part of the hedge, its branches heavily laden with white, frothy-looking flowers. As you get nearer you can smell the distinctive scent of the elder flowers and you can hear the gentle buzzing of bees and other insects as they forage for nectar. In fact, the drone of bees lulls you into an altered state of awareness, and in this altered state you see there is a stone dolmen in the bank at the foot of the elder with enough space for you to pass through, which you do, without a moment's hesitation, followed closely by your animal guide. You touch the cold, smooth stone of the dolmen as you pass through and find yourself in front of an altar covered in a green cloth and decorated with elder flowers and a burning candle. Sitting in a circle in front of the altar are twelve figures glowing with an other-worldly light. These are the shining ones, the Elders who have each carried the wisdom of an assigned tribe through the ages: the twelve tribes that came out of Atlantis. You are drawn to one Elder in particular and, as if by telepathy, this Elder stands up and motions for you to come and sit beside him on his left. Then everyone holds hands and you feel a current of energy flow through you, passing clockwise around the circle. Take time to connect with the circle of Elders and receive their wisdom.

You realize you have fallen asleep and that the Elders have gone. There is just you and your animal guide sitting on the floor. Time has gone by and the candle has gone out. As you slowly come to, you feel a profound sense of inner peace. You stand up and make your way back out, through the dolmen and along the ancient trackway with your animal ally, feeling blessed with the wisdom that has been shared with you, as you return to your tree.

Evening Primrose ~ love from Venus

There is something extraordinarily beautiful about the flowers of evening primrose. They seem to glow with an inner light. The oil extracted from its seeds have been used for generations for a variety of health and beauty purposes.

When I connect to this plant I receive the words, 'soft, gentle and patient'. She tells me she is connected to the planet Venus. On connecting to evening primrose, I see a lady in full-blown skirts of soft lemon yellow, just like the petals of the flower. She enters my consciousness and then settles down, arranging the petals of her skirt around her and patiently waits for my 'monkey mind' to stop. She says:

Venus' light is shining brightly at this time, flowing into the hearts of humanity, raising consciousness and awakening the Venus

*within. Connect to me and bathe in my radiance, breathing me into
your heart. Come home to the flower within you and wake up to the
truth that we are all love.*

I then received the impulse to repeat the affirmation 'I awaken Venus
within' three times, and I involuntarily took a huge breath and felt
myself relax into the beauty and love that is Venus.

Fern ~ adaptation

I absolutely adore ferns and so I have included some general information
on them.

Ferns appeared 50 million years ago. Along with cycad palms, they
were the only plants for millions of years and the source of our fossil
fuel today. More than 12,000 species have been identified, although
there may be up to 20,000 in existence and they can be found in all
continents except Antarctica, adapting to live in a variety of conditions—from mountains at high altitude to desert and water. Some fern
species can live for up to 100 years and can absorb heavy metals from
the soil and from the air. Ferns reproduce through releasing spores
which then develop into heart-shaped gametophytes which carry both
sperm and egg. Once fertilized, they eventually develop into a new
fern frond. Spores are so tiny that they are mainly dispersed by the
wind and can survive suspended in the atmosphere, in both heat and
light, for long periods of time, travelling great distances. The fern tells
me that the spirit of the fern that is inherent within the spore retreats
to a spiritual dimension, yet is still linked to that spore and descends
once again when environmental conditions are favourable.

The fern's message is one of adaptation: to get in touch with our
ever-evolving dreams as we embody more and more light that is now
available to us, and to make changes to our life accordingly.

We live in a constantly changing, ever-evolving environment and yet
we cling to our old ways of being, even when it does not serve us. The
fern challenges us to look at our lives with objectivity. What depletes
your energy? What no longer brings you joy? Can you redesign your

day-to-day, week-to-week routine to better serve you and the current conditions that prevail? What foods leave you feeling heavy? What new foods beckon you? What new activities are calling you which would better nourish your soul?

Let go of all that stands in your way to adapting to these current times of intense, mass spiritual awakening and the resulting chaos—and yet keep in mind that these global changes are mostly portrayed in the media in a negative, fear-based way. Much depends on individual perception based on how 'awake' we are.

Adaptation does not mean to conform. It means using our unique talents to live the life we came here to lead, inspiring others to do the same. Adapting to change is being in the present moment, constantly checking in with our hearts' desires as guided forward by our soul, in gratitude and love.

The fern also warns us against impulsivity and teaches that pre-meditated changes are best, taking into account the seasons, the cycles of the moon and the stars. Changes made in accord with the natural rhythm of life will endure. Changes made on impulse may be transient and lead us along a more meandering life-path.

So, in heart-centred awareness call forth the highest spiritual form of the fern and ask: 'What adaptations do I need to make to my life in order to be/remain in alignment with my true nature?' Let images, thoughts, words or colour come into your conscious awareness.

Forget-me-not ~ humanity's celestial origins

The flower faery of the forget-me-not looked so surprised at being addressed! She remained silent for a while, blinking, wide-eyed and innocent. She told me she liked to lighten up dark places in the garden with sparkles of heavenly blue—the blue of heaven. The deva of forget-me-not (who carries the blueprint of all forget-me-not plants) told me the plant connects earth to the heavens above and to 'Hollow Earth' within. As above, so below, as within, so without. This plant's medicine is to remind humanity of our celestial origins—that we are made of stardust!—creating a rainbow bridge between earth energy and celestial energy. When we set eyes on a cloud of forget-me-nots, it lifts our spirits, gladdens our hearts, reminding us of our spiritual nature. It changes our focus, if we allow it, to loftier matters and brings an element of the blue ray into our garden. The heavenly blue of the flower reminds us we are here to create our personal heaven-on-earth, according to our own unique gifts and talents; to manifest spirit on earth. It also reminds us that heaven is here now, in our hearts, and that we don't need to go anywhere to connect to a state of love and oneness. This heavenly state of bliss can be made manifest on earth. It is especially important to be reminded of this after the long dark winter months of introspection and dreamtime.

Foxglove ~ fae portal

Foxgloves carry the 'old magic'. For millennia, the foxglove has been favoured by the fae as a portal of choice between their realm and ours. This is because the foxglove's energy, when viewed, spirals upwards, raising in vibration those who can travel this way—in other words, those who have been initiated into the faery realms and have been given a key. So, when travelling to the faery realm from ours, it can be described as 'spiralling-up' in a silver stream of energy, not a 'stepping through'. Sometimes these are seen as spiral steps.

The right foxglove should be chosen, as many act as decoys. There are only a handful of portals in any given area and, if one possesses 'the sight', they are seen to glow. Once you enter the portal, you often first come to a 'middle land' before you enter the faery realm proper. It is very easy to get lost here as it is steeped in enchantment and is designed to keep out those who accidentally stumble upon a portal—so clearly it is advisable to travel with your faery guardian or Queen Maeve and, as you leave, always retrace your footsteps exactly. From here one must then find another access point, such as a trunk of a tree, to enter faery land proper, which is vaster than earth and comprised of many kingdoms. Again, it is important to travel with a guide who knows which part of the faery realm you wish to go to. There is a part of the faery realm where our faery guardians reside, which can be an interesting place to visit.

Let foxgloves grow where their seed falls. You can be sure a faery will be looking after the germinating seed. Foxgloves favour dappled shade and moist soil. They will grow in drier conditions, but not to their full potential. Allow yourself to be surprised at colour variations, which often the faeries themselves have had a hand in.

Hawthorn Flowers ~ embrace sexuality

Embrace your sexuality as a sacred path to the divine.

The ascended spirit of the hawthorn appears as a tall lady dressed in white, with hawthorn flowers around her head and an upturned crescent moon on her forehead. She also wears a girdle of hawthorn flowers crossing her sacral area. She drops hawthorn flowers, which I must place my feet upon as I follow her to a luminous sacred space. I see her turn to face me and draw the star-fire magic of hawthorn flowers down into a bowl, which then becomes a sacred white flame which she holds cupped to her sacral. She then places it into my sacral and healing occurs.

> *So many of you are cut off from your sexuality and yet this is such a sacred part of you and a gateway to the divine. Hold hawthorn flowers to your sacral chakra or make a girdle of hawthorn flowers and breathe in from this chakra the white star-fire flame of hawthorn, holding the intention of healing your sexuality, your sensuality.*
>
> *My berries provide healing for affairs of the heart, releasing emotional congestion from the heart chakra. The magic of hawthorn berries allows you to see deeper and to become aware of the other's point of view, and gifts you with awareness of that which you have projected onto the other. In doing so, you have the opportunity to reclaim that which you have denied within yourself, returning yourself to wholeness.*

The spirit of the hawthorn also told me that hawthorn is one of the favoured portals between our world and the fae, especially at Beltane/ May Day in days gone by, when this was a time for love rites. This is because the fae had been drawn to the physicality of humans' lovemaking. This is why it has been recorded in our mythology that the fae entered into relationships with humans in order to experience this. In their dimension they live for hundreds of years and rarely need to procreate, but when they do it is by a blending of energies.

Journey to meet the Spirit of the Hawthorn

First, follow the relaxation technique already described on p. 87 (in the section on 'Journey to meet the spirit of the elder'). Call in your animal guide and find yourself on an ancient trackway lined either side by a dense tall hedge of spindle, holly, guelder rose and hawthorn. This trackway has an otherworldly feel. The hedge is teeming with life, home to myriad forms both physical and energetic—such as nature spirits, gnomes and flower faeries. As you walk along with your animal ally, you feel the magic of this leafy green track and you sense that it has been in use for hundreds of years as a processional faery way. Hear the birdsong, listen to the bees humming, the rustle of leaves. This is a spirit road. A faery path.

Now, suddenly, low down in a hawthorn tree, your eyes catch sight of a beautiful nest. In the nest you spy three pale blue-speckled eggs. Then you see something else, glinting in the nest. Under the watchful eye of the mother blackbird, who is close by, you reach in to the nest, marvelling at the soft, mossy interior and retrieve the golden object. It is a tiny key. You step back and turn round, holding the key up to the sun, noticing that etched on its surface are tiny glyphs—ancient symbols. Then you turn back around and see that a door has appeared in the trunk of the hawthorn tree with a keyhole to match the key. You realize this doorway is just big enough to crawl through and so you place the key in the keyhole and slowly turn it. It swings open and, getting down on your hands and knees, you crawl through after your animal ally. And then you gasp. You enter what only can be described as a much larger space than is possible from a logical perspective. This magical space allows you to stand up and, looking around you and then up above you, you see this space is made up of hawthorn branches, tightly interlaced, forming walls and an arched ceiling above you. It feels sacred and the floor is made up of hundreds of hawthorn flowers. You breathe in their intoxicatingly heavy scent and, sitting down, you pick one up, feeling its tiny silky petals and noticing its delicate stamens.

Shafts of sun suddenly reach through between the hawthorn branches, illuminating the hawthorn blossom in your hand and lighting up the blossom floor beneath you. It is a magical moment. Then you see a ribbon of silver light weaving in the air before you, and you sense a silky, fluid quality. You realize this is the spirit of the hawthorn. See her now. She will appear to you as an image borrowed from your subconscious. Introduce yourself and say that you would love to learn from her or receive healing, and in return ask what you can do for her. Take time to commune with the spirit of the hawthorn.

Thank the spirit of the hawthorn and crawl back through the door, accompanied by your animal ally. Lock the door and slip the key back into the nest, under the feathery breast of the mother blackbird, who calmly watches you with her beady eye. Then return along the ancient trackway, back to your tree.

In your own time, open your eyes and come back to your normal waking reality.

Heather ~ purification of boundaries

Heather's medicine is the purification of boundaries. I feel its association with luck is by virtue of its purification properties. When requested, it can burn away lower and unwanted energies from entering your auric field, so it's good to carry a piece. Likewise, a pot of heather placed outside of your front door will purify the boundary to your home. The fae love heather and have a long-entwined history with its spirit. They say:

> Our love of heather springs from an alliance we made long ago. We tend to it in your world, often by making people feel unwelcome in the wild and untamed places where heather grows, so it can remain undisturbed and our portals undiscovered. In return, heather helps us keep the boundaries betwixt and between our world and yours pure, preventing unwanted energies crossing over.

I was then shown an image of a plume of heather surrounded by fire with a doorway within. In areas where there is no heather, the fae use foxglove as portals between our worlds, and the foxglove's energy spiral—see foxglove plant message—has the same effect of leaving behind lower energies.

Hellibore (Lenten Rose) ~ empowerment

The words I first received from the Lenten rose deva and faery were, 'queenly', and 'crown'. I then connected to a much darker energy, and the Lenten rose explained that it had been unfairly labelled as being dark and causing injury. *'We have been used to cause harm, which is not our true nature.'* When I researched this, it transpires that the roots contain a poison which is an emetic and laxative and that it was given to children to purge worms which sometimes caused fatalities. The energy then lightened and it went on to say:

> *Our true nature is one of empowerment and sovereignty. I connect you to your crown chakra, to your sovereignty, to your truth. Stand tall and proud and shine your light upon the world, even when all seems dark. Each and every one of you makes a difference.*

'Supremacy' was another word given to me by the Lenten rose. To have supremacy over oneself is to master oneself—taking care of oneself and forming an appropriate relationship to oneself and others, which then reveals your truth. In turn, truth stands in circular relationship to power. Being in your power, expressing your truth, in turn reinforces your power. You can choose to have a positive influence in peoples' lives by sharing your truth to those to whom it resonates with.

Honeysuckle ~ soul nourishment

How many of us have smelled the intoxicating heady scent of honeysuckle on a warm summer's evening? This plant really takes me back to my childhood, and the fae tell me they too adore the plant.

Honeysuckle 'medicine' connects us back to the sweetness of life, to the essence of what makes us feel good and nourishes our soul. This will be different for each individual. In heart-centred awareness, connect to a honeysuckle in your garden, or hold a piece in your hand and ask, 'What truly nourishes my soul?' Let the answer come in words, images or a deep knowing. True soul nourishment brings you to a place of being at one with your divinity, with feelings of deep peace and inner contentment.

A popular planting combination for your garden is a rose with honeysuckle entwined. These plants will then hold the qualities of love and soul nourishment, the synergy of which is pure bliss!

Iris Reticulata* ~ eye of the storm

My wisdom for you at this time is to enter the eye of the storm. Just intend and it will be so. In this energetic space, all is calm and quiet. All extraneous influences and the chaos of the collective consciousness fall away. It is where you can be at one with the god/dess. Know which issue, for you personally, has surfaced to be addressed at this potent time of the impending new moon/solar eclipse.* The eye of the storm is where magic and alchemy occur. This is where the rainbow bridge of understanding and healing can be found. Just intend to be in this energetic space and connect to the god/dess/Source from your heart and then ask what issue you need to address and it will surface as a word, an image or a deep knowing. You can then ask how to resolve and heal this issue. Know that by working on yourself you are affecting the collective consciousness of humanity, adding to its light/enlightenment. Also know that, when we return to the higher dimensions of light and love, there are no lessons to be learned. All just 'is'. Now is the time to make the choice to fully connect to your higher dimensional self and be the truth of who you are. Many of you are fluctuating between 3D† and higher dimensions and this is impacting on your health and vitality. The light and love is now available to you here on the earth plane. Connect with it from your heart-space and

---

* Iris can be called upon at any time that we need to feel centred and peaceful.

† 3D represents a level of light/vibration that resonates with the material world of fear, separation and duality.

intend to remain in a fifth-dimensional state.* Support this intent by regularly bringing in the light and love with joy-filled activities and states of being.

The spiritual wisdom of plants and indeed all of Nature is here to support you in these times of great change. Your challenge is to be still in Nature and connect from your heart-space. Blessed be.

Ivy ~ higher connection

This is a message received at Samhain/Halloween (Celtic New Year). Pan, god of Nature, showed me an ivy crown and told me that ivy was sacred to him.

You are always connected through your crown chakra to the cosmos, to your guides, to your higher self, soul, monad[†] and Source. This higher guidance means you need never feel lost and alone. In heart-centred awareness, ask me, Pan, god of Nature, to place an ivy crown around your head. Ask the spirit of ivy in its highest form to connect with you. Then allow imagery or words or pure knowing, to heal and guide you on the next steps of your journey. Blessed be.

Wear your ivy crown for all to see,
At one with the cosmos, the plants and the trees.
Embrace Pan, god of Nature's sacred laws
Of love and oneness, opening doors
spiralling ever closer to your divinity within
Honouring the Celtic new year—
a magical time to begin.

---

* Fifth dimension is a level of light/vibration resonating with unconditional love, abundance and oneness.

† Monad is the divine, immortal part of our spiritual spark (or individualized Spark of God/dess).

Japanese Anemone ~ grace

When linking with the spirit of the Japanese anemone, the phrase 'state of grace' was given to me. It said:

> *Be graceful in all of your dealings. To be graceful is a strength. In these tumultuous times of ascension, the art of being graceful is of huge benefit in that it conserves your energy and keeps you relaxed and centred. When a perceived difficulty presents itself, take a step back, go into your heart-space and ask, 'How can I best honour myself and serve the other person'. To approach a situation in this way is to be in a state of grace. You are connecting to the divinity within and thus more able to receive higher guidance for all concerned.*

Lavender ~ tranquillity

Everyone can find space for a patch of lavender in their gardens! Loved by humanity for centuries and adored by bees and other pollinating insects, lavender is relaxing and yet uplifting, is peaceful and yet gives us clarity. It invokes tranquillity, helping us to drop out of our busyness and into our 'beingness'. Part of lavender's magic is to reconnect us to our divinity; its scent bringing us into the present moment.

> *I soothe, I calm, I heal. I am also a facet of the violet ray—transmuting negativity and facilitating you to become all that you can be, so that you may help to usher in the new age of enlightenment. I will lift you to a place where your truth resides, reconnecting you to your divinity within, so that you may step out into the world with a renewed perspective, rooted in a calm state of 'beingness'. I also carry the silver ray, which on the physical plane is antibacterial and antifungal and on the spiritual plane connects you to the moon's tides and rhythms of Nature.*

The fae love lavender too, especially its connection to the silver ray and the moon. The Sidhe/magical fae of Danaan, a faery race found in Scotland and Ireland, wear cloaks of light woven with ribbons of light taken from the plant kingdom, including that of lavender. This helps them to be at one with Nature and balances their etheric bodies, protecting them from our dimension's current imbalances. This cloak of light facilitates their passage through Nature's realms, allowing them to travel between the worlds. Many moons ago, in Lemurian and Atlantean times, we could do this too with the fae's help, and this facilitated our understanding of all of Nature's kingdoms at a spiritual level/energetic level, so that we could co-create in harmony. We are fast approaching these times again, of reconnection to the spiritual realm of Nature. We do this by carrying an increased quotient of light (ascension) and through our reconnection to the fae races and their timely wisdom. Then we will truly understand the impact we are having on Mother Nature and what we must do to remedy it.

Lime Tree ~ rest & enjoyment

A summer solstice message:

> My message to you is the importance of rest, relaxation and enjoyment. Take time to carve out from your busy schedule regular time to relax and connect with what brings you joy.
>
> In a society that measures success based on achievements and titles, this can be a challenge for many of you, but know it is just as important to be as to do. Many of you feel guilty if you take time out to rest, relax and have fun. This makes no sense. Relaxation allows your batteries/adrenals to recharge, which is fundamental to your overall health and well-being. In the expansive state of relaxation, the whispers of your soul can be heard as well as the wisdom of your body and what it needs for health. Your original promise to the god/dess was to embody love and joy and express this love and joy in your own unique way. So make time for joyful soul nourishing activities, rest and relaxation. And know that in doing so, you are giving the next person permission to do so, and the next and the next... like ripples in a pond, initiating change, one person at a time. Much love and blessings.

Meadowsweet ~ love thy neighbour

Also called Bridewort and Queen of the Meadow.

Many is the time we judge. This strikes a blow, energetically speaking. It places us in dis-harmony, in a state of dis-grace. Making false assumptions, we detach from the flow of the goddess, from her love, from her light.

Them and us. You and me. Separation and distrust. The world becomes a shadowland. We fear, lash out, blame and condemn. This is not the way forward.

Let me teach you to embrace another. Hold sacred space as they present themselves, their views, their visions. In neutrality, in heart-centred awareness, we listen, honouring 'another me'. Keep what resonates. Discard that which causes you discord.

Being the light of your truth does not mean cutting others down. It means holding this light in your heart and expressing it with heartfelt peaceful action within your own life.

Be the change you seek, but always with love. Call upon me when you have fallen out of love with life. I will bring you home to that sweet place in your heart, completing the circle once again. Blessed be.

Morning Glory ~ honour your divinity

Nature is ascending at a faster rate than humanity. By gazing upon the beauty of Nature you will be facilitating your ascension process—your enlightenment.

I am Ipomoea, morning glory, and I offer you my light, my love. I am here to remind you of your star origin. I work on your third eye and crown chakra and transpersonal chakras* above the crown, to reconnect you to your celestial origin. A stronger connection with home will help you with your enlightenment and soul's impulse for being here. With heart-centred awareness, gaze on me and call forth your celestial origin through me. Sit in this energy and ground it, deep into Mother Earth. That is all that is required. Namaste.

---

* Chakras found above the head.

The growth habit of this plant spirals up through other plants, mimicking the ascending spiral dance of enlightenment.

Motherwort (leonurus cardiaca) ~ courage

Much has been written about me as I have a long history entwined with yours (humanity's). Indigenous to the British Isles, I am sacred to the goddess and in my highest vibration the goddess works through me. In matriarchal times the healing arts were sacred and were the domain of women. I was honoured at your altars, along with other herbs, and my spirit was invoked in sacred space before remedies were prepared. When men took over they did not care to work in this way, misunderstanding that the potency then was greatly reduced when the spiritual was overlooked.

For those who wish to connect with me, heart to heart, know I am the Lion Mother goddess and will fiercely protect and nurture you so that you have the courage to be who you are in the world, to be courageous in expressing your truth.

In heart-centred higher awareness, express your truth authentically and with love. The time is NOW for your sacred work.

Call on me for heart and sacral-chakra healing and my all-encompassing love.

With my first contact, I saw the spirit of the motherwort clad in robes of olive green and gold. She appeared to me as a bountiful mother goddess holding sheaves of wheat. When I connected with her a second time she was very leonine and golden and gave me a beautiful heart healing.

Mugwort (artemesia vulgaris) ~ heart of the matter

Artemesia works within the realms of emotions bringing forth that which needs to come to light and is sacred to the goddess Artemis and to the goddess Cerridwen.

When you wish to see to the heart of the matter, I am your herb. I will help you to descend into your shadow and bring forth illumination to the answers you seek. Know that the only true path is the spiral. It leads you into the centre of your heart—the core of your being. Do not waste time with outer-world distractions. Seek all of the answers inside of yourself through meditation, dreamwork and quiet contemplation, calling me in as your ally. This is the free-flowing path of the goddess. Know thyself, both dark and light. With me by your side you need fear nothing. In reclaiming your shadows, fear loses its power, diminishing little by little with each descent until you uncover a light so bright that you become a beacon for the world. Everyone must do this work for your world to change and become more peaceful, loving and united in sisterhood/brotherhood.

I am of 'Nine Herbs Charm'* (assigned to the goddess). I am Artemesia.

Ways to work with this powerful plant ally are to meditate with some of the dried herb whilst soaking in a bath, burn it in a charcoal burner or sleep with it under your pillow. You can also make a tea with it by infusing one teaspoon of the herb in boiling water for ten minutes. Do not work with it if you are pregnant as it stimulates the uterus.

Nettle (urtica dioica) ~ reclaim your wild nature

I see the spirit of the nettle as tall and green pulsating with golden light.

I grow freely in wild places and my message to you in these times is to give yourself permission to reclaim your wild nature. This is an intrinsic part of who you are but societal 'norms' have caused you to suppress this part of you for such a long time that you may not even recognize it. By reclaiming your wild nature and stepping out of your self-imposed and societal constraints, your ideas and inspirations

---

* An old English charm to aid the wounded, which involves the preparation of nine plants, including mugwort.

will encompass new possibilities of being and doing and then true progress can be made by humanity 'thinking outside the box'. It is especially beneficial to connect with me if you feel you are stagnating in any area of your life. In reconnecting you to your wildness, I will open you up to new possibilities of living your life in a way never considered before.

You can connect to the nettle by being in your heart's space and inviting the spirit of the nettle to step forward. Alternatively, you can drink nettle tea (1 tablespoon of dried nettle in a cup of boiling water and steep for 15 minutes)* and again call forth the spirit of the nettle and ask it to connect you to your wild nature. It is important that you follow any impulses that support freeing your spirit, and maybe even intend to do one thing that you consider wild for you each day or week!

It is also important to leave a portion of your garden wild for nettles to grow if you can, as this is such an important food for caterpillars and subsequently butterflies and moths. This will delight the fae too!

Oak ~ strength of conviction

When I link with the energy of the oak I see golden light and the words 'mighty' and 'majestic' come to mind. The spirit of the oak says:

Call upon me when you need strength of conviction. For anything you are undertaking, I can provide the energy and power to see it through to completion.

Indeed the electrical current of the oak is far higher than any other tree.† I was shown in meditation that in days gone by people would bury small bags of coins at the foot of venerated oak trees to ensure

---

* Contraindications: nettle shouldn't be given to pregnant women as it can stimulate uterine contractions. It also shouldn't be used whilst taking lithium, diuretics, diabetes medications, sedatives, blood thinners, or blood pressure medications, or if you have low blood pressure or inflammation of the kidneys/nephritis.

† See *The Spirit Of Trees*, by Fred Hageneder.

success in an endeavour. The oak carries both sexes on the same tree and so either energy can be accessed, depending on what one needs.

The oak has a strong taproot and so, when we connect to the oak, this deep grounding enables us to then soar high with our aspirations. When working magically with trees, I feel the Druids, as well as working with the basic forces of Nature, also connected to the planets within our cosmos. For oak, this would be Mars and its creative male energy, and this planetary connection causes the oak's unique zigzag growth and strong taproot as well as the lobed leaf shape. The spirit of the oak also offers protection and indeed is home to myriad life forms, both physically and etherically.

The 'Oaken Halls of Magic' is a sacred place we can be granted access to in times of great need. It is a place of sanctuary and restoration, of renewal and regeneration; a place where clarity can be sought. It is a place of great vitality that awaits our 'dream seeds' and then clarifies them for us so that only the most heartfelt ones are germinated. We can present our dream seeds and be shown by the great oak king spirit whether they are truly in alignment with our soul. If we are not sure of our heartfelt dreams, we can ask to be shown them. Once we are shown the potential of our dream seeds, they can then be germinated here and the magic of the oak will provide the vitality to bring them to fruition. The Oaken Halls of Magic are accessed through a yoni (womb)-shaped gap in the trunk of a great oak tree. Once inside, we are led through a series of arches made of polished oak into the great oaken hall. The oak is so highly polished that it shines, and a beautiful golden-warm glow suffuses this sacred space. So how do we find this sacred place? It is as simple as asking. Ask in meditation or, if you prefer to journey there, ask your 'power animal'* to lead you. Then just sit in the energy of the great oak king and present your dreams. As humans we do over-complicate things, so just sink into your heart-space, out of the judgemental mind, and allow this magic to happen.

---

* In shamanism it is believed everyone has a 'power animal' who acts as a guardian and guide. The shaman moves between a three-tiered universe, an upper-world, middle-world and lower-world, all connected by a great tree.

Omphalodes cappadocica ~ *authentic self-expression*

Be the light of your authentic self-expression.

Your passionate and authentic creativity is called for right now for the collective enlightenment of humanity. It is crucial to create the time and space for this.

Queen Maeve of the fae says:

Many, many moons ago, plants spoke to humanity, just as you remember that the trees spoke to the Druids. Man listened with his heart and not his mind. Indeed, man listened to all of the kingdoms of Nature and took guidance from the wisdom received. Man was part of Nature and did not seek dominion over it. In these goddess societies of old, feelings were honoured in partnership with the intellect. Being in your heart-space is crucial now to your evolution and enlightenment. Continually bring yourselves back to this heart-centred feeling state throughout the day until it is your default mode of being. Only then will answers be found to your current challenges, both individually and collectively.

I am Queen Maeve of the fae and I will impart my wisdom to anyone who calls upon me. Blessed be.

Orchid ~ *illuminating your path back to the divine*

Orchids are ancient flowers of great beauty that are unsurpassed in the level of divine light they hold. They carry codes of exquisite light and love to re-awaken humanity.

They are one of the two largest families of flowering plants (the other being *asteraceae*) numbering more than 28,000 species. They are thought to have originated 100 million years ago.

The orchid's consciousness is highly evolved and originates from stars such as Sirius, maintaining connections with evolved planets and star systems.

We are sacred earth keepers and we carry the codes for the new sacred earth and the ascension of all kingdoms upon her. We wish to work with humanity in a more conscious way at this time. The plant kingdom has always been your ally, even though in more modern times the majority have forgotten this. We wish to co-create the new world with you, facilitating both inner transformation and planetary transformation. Our consciousness is vast and highly-evolved. Do not underestimate the guidance and healing we can offer you on your earth walk. Consult us in all matters, just as the Sirians do in their healing gardens. We are pure channels to the divine.

I have been given this pathway to meet the spirit of orchid:

Go in to your heart-space and see a rainbow bridge. Cross this bridge into an enchanted forest. Use all of your senses to find yourself there. The colours seem vivid and other-worldly. Start to walk through the forest until you come to a green pyramid made of quartz with chlorite. Enter this pyramid and see many levels within it, full of orchids of many colours and shapes. Each level is connected by escalators seemingly made of light. The different levels do not indicate a hierarchy of orchids. You notice shining figures tending to them. Ask your higher self to show you the orchid you need to connect with and stand in front of it, allowing its energy to pour into your heart chakra for as long as you feel guided to do so. Then ask it for any guidance you need at this time in your life. When you are ready, retrace your steps, back over the rainbow bridge, into your heart-space, and then return to normal waking reality.

The International Flower Essence Repertoire has a beautiful set of orchid cards which can be used as an oracle and to energetically connect with your chosen orchid. They also make orchid essences.[*]

Peony ~ strength in vulnerability

The peony's medicine is 'strength in vulnerability'. It has fragile petals that if exposed to the wind and rain shortens the life of the bloom, and yet this does not stop it flowering because, like all plants, it is strongly

---

[*] See www.healingorchids.com

rooted in its nature. It knows this is what it is here to do and just puts out more flowers!

When we bring our gifts to the world we can feel vulnerable, exposed, open to ridicule—even dismissed. Yet by connecting to our true nature, in service to the divine, this brings us feelings of deep fulfilment and peace. We feel grounded, centred and whole. The vulnerability we feel is fear-based and arises from the ego/mind, and as such is an illusion. The truth is that we are loved and supported every step of the way. The peony gently opens our hearts to an exquisite love that is both gentle and strong. Rest in the spirit of the peony and heal your feelings of vulnerability. In doing so, watch a strength emerge and a commitment to bring forth your gifts for the benefit of all.

Red clover (trifolium pratense) ~ find your passion

Spirit of Clover
Fire of trine
reveal to me my passion
my heartfelt, unique design.

Many, many moons ago, Queen Danu came to the land we now know as Ireland and she brought her people with her, in present times known as the Magical Fae Of Danaan or Sidhe. It is said they journeyed by shape-shifting into swans, flying across the seas from the land we now call Iceland, and brought with them their magic. They were the shining ones, tall in stature, and they created cities of light, living in harmony with the land and all the kingdoms upon her. Clover was a sacred plant to them, containing the fire of inspiration and of passion. Queen Danu (later to be deified) and her people flourished in their cities of light for hundreds of years until the human barbarians came, bringing with them their warfaring and brutal ways. These barbarians tried to conquer them so Queen Danu took counsel and retreated to the Hollow Hills, an alternate dimension of earth, leaving behind many myths and legends about the Sidhe and of clover. In truth, clover carries the fire element trine, the sacred flame of life which can ignite your soul's passion, that is, your *raison d'être* for being on this present earth walk. Connect to the spirit of the clover and ask what is your soul's passion, or if you already know, then ask to be shown a deeper understanding.

Rose ~ unconditional love

I am the spirit of the rose and I originally came to you from Venus. The rose has a long history entwined with yours and has a special place in your hearts—the heart of humanity. It is a reminder of home—a place of pure unconditional love, peace and harmony, where there is no striving, just being. There are many stories and myths surrounding the rose from the dawn of your recent history but there is one unfolding right now which is most relevant to you. As Gaia ascends, the over-lighting faery of the rose is evolving into a goddess in her own right. She is yet another facet to the diamond face of the goddess. The rose faery is transforming into the rose goddess to assist humanity's ascension process, attuning each and every one of you to the pure unconditional love of the goddess and her qualities of love, cooperation and co-creativity, and her blessings of peaceful, harmonious communities linked across the face of the world. The rose is also a gateway to the goddess Sophia, Queen of the Heavens, who originates from Alcyone, (our Great Central Sun in the Pleiades, where all of our Source energy for the ascension process comes from and is stepped down through our sun). This is because Sophia has sent a cosmic impulse down to earth which has triggered a corresponding impulse within the seed of life codes, allowing the rose to become this gateway to her. As above, so below.

Connect with the rose faery goddess regularly, placing your consciousness in your heart-space and watch your energy soar, as it fills with pure unconditional love. Then direct it out into every cell of your being, into each of your subtle energy bodies, mental, emotional and spiritual, and then beyond to bless the world. You can also ask the rose goddess to take you to the fountain of life within your sacred heart and there you can taste the 'waters of heaven'. This connects you to the very heart of your being where revelations can occur, helping you evolve back to yourself.

The rose in my garden is many years old. It is very tall and tells me it is the head plant of the garden and orchestrates all of the individual plants' energies. I saw all of the energies drawing into the rose and then flowing out in an organized manner, resulting in an overall focused, cohesive 'whole'. If there is no head plant in a garden, then the overall energy of it is more discordant. I was told my myrtle is waiting in the wings to take over this role when the rose comes to the end of its life.

Rose of Sophia meditation

Use the visualization process on p. 87. Look for a way to journey to the upper world. You might want to climb your tree with your animal, or fly with them or climb a ladder or steps that miraculously appear by you. And up and up you go. Higher and higher, higher and higher still, until you start to pass through the clouds—and still you go higher until the light takes on a different quality, more luminous, more ethereal. And there before you appear magnificent golden gates. You pass through them and find yourself in a rose garden; roses of every colour for as far as the eye can see. You reach out and touch the petals of a rose, silky smooth beneath your fingertips. The air is rich with their scent and you feel intoxicated, breathing in the perfume and allowing it to relax you. Deeply relaxed, you look for a soft place to lie down beneath one of the rose bushes. Lying down now, you close your eyes and start to breathe in and out through your heart chakra; in through your heart and out through your heart, in and out, feeling your heart chakra gently expanding. In your mind's eye, your heart becomes a white rose with the palest of pink edging, with many, many, intricately laced petals, softly curled. And you start to sink into this rose, sinking and sinking, deeper and deeper into your heart rose, deep into your sacred heart. You find yourself standing in a chamber of crystalline light, deep within you, deep within the very essence of your being. All around you is soft white light, even though you cannot see its source. The light glows, pulsates. You feel deeply calm, relaxed, with a sense of expansion, of being at home in the truest sense of the word. And a being of glistening bright light now steps forward and stands in front of you. She is Sophia, goddess of deep soul-wisdom and faith. She bears in her hands a rose made of white light, so bright you can hardly look at it, and she places this rose into your heart. You feel crystalline codes of light radiating out through every level of your being, moving through your four bodies,* radiating out like ripples in a pond. You breathe deeply as you ensoul this wisdom that Sophia is imparting to you, feeling it nourish you at every level. You feel a veil of amnesia being lifted from you, softly melting with Sophia's deep love for you; deep unconditional love as you connect more deeply to your truth, to your true nature, your authentic self. You place your hand on her heart, as her hand is on yours, and you find yourself breathing as one, gazing into her eyes as this happens, feeling a deep sense of love—unconditional love—enveloping you. And be still now and receive guidance from Sophia, guidance for your earthly walk. This guidance may come to you as pictures, as symbols, or as a knowing. Gradually you become aware of being back in the rose garden, becoming aware of the scent of roses again, and you stretch and stand up.

Your power animal stands before you, and together you leave the garden through the golden gates and slowly descend back down to the earth plane. Down and down you go, down and down through the clouds, finding your feet on the ground and hugging your tree, feeling it solid against your body. You thank your power animal and slowly open your eyes, becoming fully present in the room.

Rowan Tree ~ transmutation & inspiration

The rowan tree is associated with the goddess Brigid and Mary Magdalene and carries the flame of transmutation and inspiration, which is most potent to call upon in the seasons of autumn and spring.

---

* We possess four bodies—a physical body, an emotional subtle energy body, a mental subtle energy body and a spiritual subtle energy body.

The first time I journeyed to meet the spirit of the rowan, I was camping in Abersoch, Wales. I was met by the 'People of Rowan', a magical race of the fae. They led me through a series of archways to a dimension where each tree's soul resides. Here the rowan soul shone and I felt it resonated to the frequency of magic, alchemy and transformation (I was shown the latter through images of one thing turning into another). At its highest frequency, I was shown the joining of the divine masculine and divine feminine and felt the love and bliss that emanated from this union.

In the season of autumn, when the rowan tree is bejewelled with scarlet berries, it offers us the chance to transmute the old into something quite new. By stepping into the rowan tree's fire of transmutation and giving up all that is holding us back from full authentic expression, we see the new arise, like a phoenix from the ashes. So just as the process of alchemy takes a base metal and turns it into gold, you can take all of the lessons learned and wisdom gained this year, from both successes and failures, and watch them turn into something quite new—a new approach if we are still passionate about our path, or an entirely new, inspired adventure. No venture has ever been wasted.

In springtime the rowan tree is adorned with white blossom and strongly associated with the goddess Brigid and her rowan arrows of inspiration. Again we can enter the rowan tree's flame of transmutation at this time, peeling off the layers we no longer need, and we can ask for the gift of inspiration and rebirth of spirit—new ideas to sow and germinate for our next cycle of creativity.

The rowan also offers us protection through its power of transmutation, especially when journeying in the otherworld. It is also a wonderful ally when using higher magic, calling upon the powers that reside in higher dimensions to effect change by guarding the threshold to the otherworld, and is often found planted at sacred sites.

So, below is a shamanic journey that I made in autumn. You are invited to step into the rowan's fire of alchemy, where you can offer up all of the year's experiences and receive a gift that is left in the smouldering embers—your gift of alchemy to inspire you in future endeavours.

Rowan Tree Journey

Once again, use the visualization process on page 87. It is night-time and a full silvery moon hangs in the dark night sky. Your spiritual ally takes you into the trunk of this tree and then you make your way down into the roots along a tunnel. You smell the damp earth as the tunnel twists and turns, this way and that, and you keep close behind your ally as it is quite dark. Then you round a bend and emerge into a landscape lit by autumnal sunshine. No sooner are you out of the tunnel than your ally starts to dig, and down you go again, into another earthy tunnel. Again it twists this way and that and again you keep near your ally as it is dark. This happens for a total of seven times, descending into the very heart of Mother.

Finally, you emerge into the light and find yourself on the outskirts of a great forest. This is no ordinary forest—it is the immortal soul of Mother Earth, a forest that glows with a gold and emerald light. A guardian stands at the entrance to this forest. He stands tall, dressed in long brown robes, and you state that you are here to connect with the spirit of the rowan tree. He stands back and your animal ally leads you into the emerald forest. The trees that surround you are incredibly tall and hundreds of years old. Some you recognize and some you don't, but all glow with an other-wordly light. And as you journey deeper and deeper, you start to see a glowing light up ahead. As you get nearer, you see an astonishing sight—a rowan tree is on fire, only this fire is not consuming it. It radiates golden orange and is quite beautiful. You are mesmerized by the flames reaching high into the sky. Your spiritual ally beckons you forwards into the flaming tree, and intuitively you know you are safe and that you must give up that which no longer serves you as you start to focus inwards with the approach of autumn. It is a time when you review your successes and failures, gleaning all of the wisdom you have learnt from both, ready to enter the dreamtime of winter. When you dream anew, some of these dreams form seeds that are ready to sow in springtime. And on and on it goes, this great glorious cycle of life. Offer to the flaming rowan tree all that you wish to let go of, and allow yourself to be surprised by other suggestions made by the spirit of the rowan, who is in communion with your soul.

And you step from the flames feeling refreshed and feeling renewed. Turning around you look back at the tree. There at the foot of the trunk is the rowan's gift of alchemy that has emerged from its flames. Your gift has significance only for you. Retrieve this gift and, if the symbolism is not obvious, ask the rowan tree for its meaning.

Thank the rowan tree and follow your animal ally out of the forest and up through each of the seven tunnels, back out to your tree that you started from. Touch the trunk. Feel your feet firmly planted on the ground here and then come back to your surroundings and normal waking reality.

Silver Birch (The Lady of the Woods) ~ unicorns & the star goddess Arianrhod

The silver birch can be found for example in Greenland, Russia and Britain and copes with wind, hard frost and strong sunshine. It is one of the first tree species to spring up in abandoned ground and nurtures new woodland with its shallow roots, which help to improve soil conditions, and its ability to let sunlight filter through its leaf canopy.

When I connect to the silver birch tree, asking its spirit to step forward in its highest vibration, I see the papery silver bark of its trunk as a column of light and the tiny fluttering leaves as dancing light.

The silver birch's energy feels nurturing and holds sacred space by bringing in light and love from Venus and the divine feminine/goddess energy. There is a beautiful silver birch on a piece of land at a school where I work, which is holding sacred space for a project to design a sensory garden for the children. I feel that once the garden has been planted, the birch will cast its light and love, filling the garden and touching the hearts of the children playing there. The unicorns and faeries also love the silver birch, being attracted to her light and soft nurturing energy.

Alphedia Arara writes in her book *Ascending with Unicorns, Activating the Heart Centre,** that unicorns are beings of divinity, bringing love and light to the planet, and that there are many different types to be found in many different galaxies and realms. Elemental unicorns can be found living in groups within silver birch woods and woods of sacred grove energy in isolated places, away from humanity. I can only describe their energy as exquisite, light and extremely gentle and loving. I met the head of one such herd, but the rest held back as they are extremely shy and cautious. This unicorn told me that elemental unicorns are guests of Mother Earth, invited here to help with their evolution (as indeed we all are) and in return they seed light and love into the earth. Elemental unicorns come and go through portals within silver birch trees, travelling between the physical earth and its etheric counterpart.

> *I am the silver birch. I connect to you in love, fully sovereign. I bring much light to the land and to humanity. To connect with me is to feel expansive, as I put you in touch with the vastness of your being—your multi-dimensional self. Know that your personality self is but one facet of the jewel that you are. Place your hand upon my trunk. This does not need to be in actual physicality; it can be in your mind's eye. Ask me to connect you to the facet of your being that will most help you on your earth walk at this time, helping you to be more of who you are, and express this in service to the divine.*

I asked for a conscious connection to a facet of myself to help me complete writing this book and immediately was aware of an elemental part of me. It felt very simple and pure in essence and connected to all of Nature. Visually I looked like a stick creature with antlers!

You could also ask the silver birch to help you connect to the unicorn realm, to visit your garden and infuse the land with love, or you could ask for help with connecting to your guardian unicorn. Alphedia Arara writes in her book that guardian unicorns reside in your aura and help with your spiritual growth. My guardian unicorn tells me that

---

* Ribble Press, eBook only.

as well as loving silver birch trees, she also loves white flowers and silvery leaves such as white sage, white roses, white rosemary and white honesty, with their gorgeous silvery seed pods. She tells me that she also loves water! It would seem inspired, then, to plant these within our gardens and to create a pond, should we wish to attract elemental unicorns or facilitate a stronger personal connection to our guardian unicorn.

The silver birch is also connected to the Welsh star goddess, Arianrhod—she who rules the Corona Borealis, or *Caer Sidi* in Welsh, the constellation of stars circling around the Pole Star in the northern sky. You can connect to Arianrhod through the silver birch in order to seek her wise counsel. To do this, first intend to connect with the highest vibration of the silver birch. See the tree as a column of white light which you step through. Find yourself on a spiral staircase. This spiral staircase of stars is like the spiral DNA helix within your cells, so that even though you are rising up, you are also simultaneously going deeper within. This feels very beautiful. Climb to the top, entering Arianrhod's revolving castle through star-clad doors. This castle is a portal connection to all of the stars within our solar system, so step through with the intention that you find yourself in the correct room, connecting to a star holding specific wisdom and/or healing for you. Or you can ask to be shown your star of origin. Arianrhod says that this connection will greatly enhance the work you are here to do.

Silver Birch, tree of light
connect me to the starry night.
Silver Birch, tree of love
connect me to the heavens above.
As above, so below
connect me to the One who knows.
Arianrhod, of starry crown
of spiral gateway
of wisdom, found.

Journey to meet the spirit of the silver birch

Once again, follow the visualization method given on p. 87. Soon you find yourself on an ancient track, lined either side by a dense tall hedge of spindle, holly, guelder rose and hawthorn. This trackway has an other-worldly feel. The hedge is teeming with life, home to myriad forms—both physical and energetic—such as Nature spirits, gnomes and flower faeries. As you walk along with your animal ally, you feel the magic of this leafy green track and you sense that it has been in use for hundreds of years as a processional faery way. Hear the birdsong, listen to the bees humming, the rustle of leaves. This is a spirit road, a faery path.

You note that the trackway curves to the left and then you see, a little way before you, a wood entirely made up of silver birch trees. It takes your breath away as it is so beautiful and seems to glow in the moonlight with an other-worldly quality. You enter into this wood. All is quiet apart from the occasional hoot of an owl, and now and again you hear the sound of a small mammal scurrying through the dried leaves at the foot of the trees.

It feels like you are expected here. You make your way through the wood with your animal guide, weaving in amongst the white papery trunks and the dancing leaves. You feel drawn on and on into the very centre of this silver birch wood. Then you catch sight of what has been drawing you in: a huge silver birch, the biggest you have ever seen, stands proud in the centre, its large trunk reflecting the silver of the moon above. You step up to this magical tree and place your hand on its trunk. It feels smooth and cold beneath your fingertips. Then you become aware of tall beings of light that telepathically convey that they are the guardians of the silver birch, and fae in origin. They beckon for you to follow them into the trunk of the tree and through a series of archways, into a different dimension. This is the place where the species of trees' overarching devas reside. They lead you to a magnificent silver birch made of pulsating, silvery light and beckon for you to sit down at the foot of this tree, with your back against the trunk. You close your eyes and sit with your animal guide in the loving and nurturing energy of the silver birch. Spend some time here, receiving healing and guidance.

When you are ready, open your eyes in this alternate dimension and see the guardians of the silver birch before you. They take your hand and help you up, leading you back through the arches, back through the original silver birch and into the wood, followed closely by your animal guide. They bow to you and you bow to them, and then they disappear.

Retrace your steps with your animal guide, through the silver birch wood and back down the spirit road, the faery path, back to your tree at the start of your journey. Gently open your eyes and come back to your normal waking state.

Snowdrop ~ purity

The gift of the snowdrop is its purity. The snowdrop reminds us to keep things pure and simple. A beautiful life is one of simplicity, shaping our thoughts, our actions, our words; where important things such as love and heart-to-heart connections take centre stage and all of the surrounding 'noise' falls away due to the lack of egoic attention. If we have cluttered minds and lead cluttered lives, we might miss the point of how precious life is. We might not see what is important and what is not.

The spirit of the snowdrop presents herself to me in a silken white skirt with lime-green edging. She holds my hand and we step into her grace—a heart healing—taking me back to my own true essence, the essence of my divinity that resides within the very heart of me. She reminds me that the divine runs through all things like a silver thread, connecting us all to the sacred web of life—we shine like drops of rain in the sun, like the pure white petals of a snowdrop.

The snowdrop also heralds spring and the promise of new beginnings. As ambassadors for the maiden aspect of the goddess Brigid, they remind us that there is always hope; that after the long cold winter, dreaming your dreams, something new will emerge.

Hope renewed,
faith restored,
fragile we emerge
to the earth's first stirring.
Smiling sweetly on the ground,
we cast our light
in fresh wonder
for this beautiful world.
May your winter's dreams emerge
as we do.
Pure inspiration.

Solomon's Seal ~ embrace your wyrd

If you are drawn to this wonderful plant, you have, in some lifetime, been an initiate in the Mystery schools, a wizard, alchemist or magician. Solomon's seal grows outside my backdoor. When the sunshine illuminates this plant first thing in the morning, it lights up the graceful arching stems, hung with clusters of white bells edged with green. The words 'majestic', 'commanding', 'strong yet graceful' are brought to mind. When connecting to the spirts of the Solomon's seal in their highest vibrations, I see tall shining ones with pointed white beards and pointed hats (taken from the imagery in my imagination—yours will be personal to you) and I know they are guardians of this planet. They are you and me in ascended forms.

> Now that the fire of Beltane has infused the land, we step forth to remind you of your sacred promise made in your lifetime(s) as an initiate and your sacred promise to care for this land. We step forth to awaken the deep magic you have within you and remembrance of your soul's contract written in the stars. Now is the time to embrace your wyrd.*

The new moon is a potent time to take this journey outlined below.

Envisage standing in front of a gateway made from the graceful arch of two stems of Solomon's seal facing each other. As you step

---

* Your fate or personal destiny.

through there are a series of arches and at each one stands a guardian of the 'old ways'. The number of arches depicts the number of lifetimes you have been an initiate. As you pass each guardian, you nod your head in acknowledgement of them and they nod in return. They are you and you are them. As you step through the last archway, intend to connect with the highest wisdom you need at this auspicious time in earth's story. Allow yourself to receive words, images, sound or colour. Allow yourself as much time as you need to fully immerse yourself and become illuminated. Then a guardian steps forward and hands you the Book of Solomon. A golden key rests upon it and you unlock its pages. They open at exactly the right page for you. The page is covered with golden symbols which start to glow, and as you trace the palm of your hand across each symbol they rise into the air and become one with you, activating your corresponding sacred codes within, awakening you to your original promise made for these times.

Toad Lilly ~ sovereignty

This is me.
This is who I Am.
I Am That I Am.

Now is the time to claim your sovereignty—your authentic personal power. This can be described as your kingly/queenly nature, whereby your crown chakra is fully activated and tuned into the stars, your soul star and the chakras beyond this, connecting you fully to your divinity—to 'All That Is'.

Nothing of any substance can be achieved without your sovereignty; there will be no real conviction that you really mean or truly believe what you say. By claiming your sovereignty you are saying, 'I am she/he and I have something to convey to the world, and it will be of substance, for this is my authenticity expressed from its highest place'.

Vervain ~ healing from the goddess

I have long been revered as a sacred herb by the ancient Egyptians, the Greeks, the Romans and by the Druids. I am a 'cure all', a mother herb, and hence dedicated to the great goddess Isis, amongst others.

I ensure all channels are light-filled, vital and free-flowing, whether in physicality or on the mental plane, ensuring open-mindedness. Or, on the spiritual plane, clearing psychic channels and opening you up to your intuition—to the voice of your soul, even to communicating with your ancestors.

I do this first and foremost by wrapping you in a cocoon of relaxation, and in this expansive state light can flow in and magic can occur at the level of body, mind or spirit. Whatever you personally need, know that it will be so.

Find comfort in the vervain's wisdom in these current challenging times, whether you imbibe her as a tea or burn the dried herb on hot charcoal or connect to her by holding a piece in your hand or over your heart.

White Rosemary ~ truth

The flower faery of the white rosemary appeared to me as a bright, white shining light. She told me that we have had a relationship with rosemary since the dawn of humanity, and revealed to me two layers of information. The first was the healing properties of rosemary as a herb. The words I received were 'stimulating', 'invigorating', 'refreshing' and 'antiseptic'. She then took me deeper into her energy and said:

You place me by your front door as a sentinel, heralding spring to all those passing by, who care to notice, who care to know. But more importantly, you place me here, signalling to the world that you are more in alignment with the truth of who you are than ever before.

She then connected me with my truth and this I feel is the gift of rosemary—she shines her light on the truth of who you are and what is true for you in any given moment. One can use this as guidance to lead a more meaningful life.

Wild Primrose ~ awakening

Mimicking the first rays of the spring sunshine
as it warms the earth,
bringing forth new life,
new growth,
we cast our soft golden light,
deep within you,
onto the seeds of your ideas,
formed during your winter slumber,
causing them to stir,
igniting the spark of creativity,
reminding you
where true fulfilment lies.

Woad (isatis tinctorial) ~ seal of completion

Also called dyer's woad and asp of Jerusalem. On connecting to this herb through a photo and holding some of its dried leaves, I heard the word 'kingly' and its presence felt incredibly strong. I feel for sure that woad is sacred to the god Woden/Odin—a Norse god of learning, poetry and magic as well as war.

Resting in my heart-space I saw needle strands of blue and received the following message:

> In essence my spiritual nature is one of completion. Knowing when to let go of the old and step into the new requires a period of contemplation and reflection in quietness and solitude. Letting go is an important process before sowing the seeds of new intentions cast at the time of Imbolc, 2 February [a spring fire festival celebrating

the return of the goddess Brigid, goddess of fire and inspiration].
A liminal space opens up between one door closing and another one opening, and it is in this indigo time of pure magic and expectation, at sunset and dawn and at the time of a blue moon [a second full moon in any given month], that it is most potent to invoke me as a 'seal' of completion. Call my spirit in at these times of betwixt and between, when true magic can occur and all of spirit and the great web of life can be felt, humming, vibrating, putting you in touch with your higher nature. Resting in your heart-space, connect with me and feel the immensity of your being and the expansiveness of your soul, calling you to a higher octave on the spiral path of life. Ask me to show you what in truth needs to end in your life in order for a new path to unfold. Then ask to be shown your soul's highest wish for you to make manifest this year. I am woad. Blessed be.

Jhenah Telyndru notes that woad was used to paint the skin of Celtic warriors blue and that this application probably had a ritual purpose. It is also used to staunch bleeding. She also adds that woad 'is used to assist in recalling past lives and is said to have been used in ancient shape-shifting rituals'.[*]

The first woad-seed finds date to the Neolithic period and Egyptians used it to dye cloth for mummies. Roman accounts, including that of Julius Caesar, describe Britons painted in blue—hence the word Picts (Latin word *Picti* meaning painted one). However, some believe that this body-painting came from copper or an iron-based pigment as modern experiences using woad have not been successful.

Wormwood (artemisia absinthium) ~ *bring to the light*

Wow—what a herb! I wouldn't recommend my first experience, though. I burnt a little of the dried herb in a charcoal burner and then I made some tea as per instructions: half a teaspoon in 250ml of boiling water and steep for 10 minutes. It was the most extreme bitter taste

---

[*] *The Avalonian Oracle* by Jhenah Telyndru (Schiffer Publishing Ltd., 2000).

I have ever had, and so I only had a tiny amount. It is worth noting here that this herb can be poisonous in large doses and should not be used in pregnancy. In the form of the drink absinthe, there is a long history of people overdosing with it—for example, plunging Van Gogh and others into madness. So, I made do with holding some of the herb and smelling it, which I found quite pleasant in comparison to its taste. I then closed my eyes in order to journey with it.

I immediately saw an older man with silver hair. He wore a cloak, carried a staff and was sitting on a throne of sorts. He then got up and plunged his staff into the ground. Immediately a white snake coiled up the staff from the ground and then, as its head appeared over the top of the staff, it opened its mouth and—much to my shock—dived into my mouth and into my body. There it looked for 'that which you would rather not see' and, as I understood it, the negative aspect of 'snake', i.e. things we hide from ourselves at the deepest level. It then shot back up and out of my mouth, expelling my darkest aspects into the light and on to the ground with a force to be reckoned with. And there, for my perusal, were several objects which jogged buried memories of long-forgotten horrors, nightmares and wretched experiences. In the main, these were childish nightmares, and I felt they had been extracted from my solar plexus (where we hold our fears).

I did not find any of this helpful or healing, so I put it to the spirit of the wormwood. I was then shown that the spirit of the wormwood has not yet ascended (Nature is ascending faster than humanity at present)—held back by its own history of misuse and the resulting fear generated. So I petitioned my guardian, Queen Maeve of the fae, and the goddess Artemisia and Source to grant ascension and, before my eyes, the snake coiled up the staff. As its head appeared over the top, it bloomed into a flower, signifying a transformation into a higher state of being. I was then told that it is important to link with this herb by calling it forth by its Latin name, *artemisia absinthium*, in order to connect with the spirit of its enlightened form. This I then did, and asked for its higher purpose.

To expel all desire to do evil. I will show you self-destructive tendencies, abuse of self and others and remove these from your holographic matrix, the part that is connected to the mind. Ancient star races, such as the Annunaki, that did not have humanity's best interests at heart, have left programmes that have interfered with your pristine true natural state of love. It is important that you do your shadow work and bring all aspects of yourself to light, because when you are hurt, the part of you that you have disowned and placed in the shadows can retaliate at a subconscious, energetic level (at its most extreme, a psychic attack). Asking me to remove these programmes will help with preventing a knee-jerk tendency to attack, born out of your shadow and mal-programming.

Finally, *artemisia absinthium* conveyed to me that the plant kingdom's spiritual evolution is closely linked to our own, and that by asking for help in this way, we facilitate its evolution. In turn, we need to clear up our environment and respect all of Nature's kingdoms, acknowledging the sacred in everything, including plants.

Yarrow ~ inner knowing

'To know me is to open a doorway to your inner knowing.'

Golden brilliance
Panicles of delight
Straight as an arrow
I will fly you to the moon of your intuition
To that which you already know is true
To that which makes you shine
Your passion
Your truth
Your service to the divine.

In order to connect with the yarrow, I drank the tea made from its dried form and also placed it on white-hot charcoal—the smell was beautiful. Then I placed it at my heart and meditated.

'What is it that you wish to know?'

I told the yarrow my dreams.

> *The course of our lives never runs true but the best we can hope for is that it meanders as a stream, seeking out the easiest route. All of your dreams will come true—but here lies the catch. Are you dreaming at all? Have you aspirations, inspirations, things that bring you exhilaration? The second sight is to see and know all things—to be betwixt and between. Let me take you there. This is a good place to manifest from.*

I was led to a doorway. Inside were many spiral staircases in all directions. There was a circle in the centre where we stood and I visualized that which I intended to manifest. Following this, the yarrow said:

> *Then let it go fully. Let all things unfurl in timely sequence. Your job is to stay heart-centred and know that which brings you joy is your divine calling and is the only way to be of true service.*

Yew Tree ~ initiation

Yew trees are renowned for their longevity and their powers of resurrection. It is said that they can live up to 3,000 years and more, and there are links between the names for yew and words for eternity. The oldest recorded yew tree is at Fortingall in Scotland and is estimated to be between 3,000 and 8,000 years old![*] There is no biological reason for a yew to die as sheaths of new bark encase old deadwood and lower branches can take root in the ground. 'A Yew that appears to be a hollow, decaying wreck is often at the beginning of its self-regeneration process.'[**]

> *Find me growing by churches, marking an ancient sacred place of power in the land. My longevity was revered in the olden days by ancient ones and, later, Druids. They knew of my role and I was revered, but this has been lost to the masses, in the antiquity of time.*

---

[*] see www.ancient-yew.org.uk

[**] See Fred Hageneder's, *The Spirit of Trees.*

The yew tree is a sacred tree of initiation, presenting a doorway to your authentic self. It can help you peel off layers of conditioning to reveal your true nature, as a much loved, divinely created being.

The following message came from a female yew tree:

> *I am the tree of death and rebirth—of transformation. My medicine for you at this time is one of renewal. Call on me if you wish to step through my doorway into a new phase of growth to take you into this coming season of winter. Winter is a time to dream of what you wish to create for the coming year. I can help you shed (like an old garment) any outmoded habits or beliefs that are holding you back—and then to dream something new into being that has true authenticity for you. May the star be at your brow, may the moon be at your belly, may the cup be at your feet. In Nature is truth. Blessed be.*

On another occasion I received this message:

> *You all have the power to rejuvenate, although humans can be quite stubborn at times, to relinquish old ideas, beliefs, habits and emotional responses. But if the call is heeded, a new phase of growth is certainly encountered. I am here to remind humanity of this and, when called upon, I can help lead you to your rebirth and can show you what stands in your way of expressing your divinity. I can then transmute the old, for you, if you are ready and willing.*

The yew is also the key into all realms, in all dimensions of time and space. Indeed, in many mythologies the 'world tree', *Yggdrasil*, is a yew tree.

> *Even though you see me physically growing in your world, I exist in all dimensions, even into the cosmos. I provide passage to many realms that you cannot even begin to conceive of in your present modern world; realms of no time, an overlapping kaleidoscope of dimensions inhabited by the fae, giants and other so-called mythical creatures—ones you know and others you have never heard of. These other realms are not necessarily more evolved than your own, just different, and some are experiencing warfare. I provide safe*

passage and a map for those entitled to traverse these realms, includ-
ing a series of sigils to enter each dimension. Journeying into these
worlds is only open to those who have a clear purpose and is not for
general curiosity. Thus, I guard these powerful portals in all dimen-
sions, locking out those uninitiated. Some of you have traversed these
realms before with the Order of Merlin. This Order is an ancient lin-
eage originating from Mur Lyon, a star existing in the cosmos. Mem-
bers of this Order have been initiated into the guardianship of this
land, its sacred trackways in this world and other realms, and the
guarding of the codes held deep within this land and beyond. Some
act as peace-makers between realms, 'maintaining the order within',
liaising with dragons and gnomes (not as you know them, but tall
wizard-like beings who maintain the flow of energy and guard codes
of wisdom). Others have been charged with retrieving wisdom from
other realms to help heal unsolvable maladies in your human world.
Many of these realms are completely closed-off to humankind, some
are evolving into higher dimensions and some contain the undead—
ancestors who have not passed over but are trapped betwixt and
between, caught through intense emotion.

Here is a journey to help you connect with the spirit of the yew and receive inner-child healing.

Use the visualization method given on p. 87. You come to a huge yew tree, its girth indicating that it's more than a thousand years old. There is an opening in the trunk which your animal ally beckons you to step through, and you find yourself in a long earthy tunnel that spirals deep down into the depths of the earth. The floor is sprinkled with yew needles and along the earthy walls are candles lighting the way. You start walking along this passageway and periodically you notice tall, cloaked figures who seem to be guarding it, stationed at intervals. The tunnel spirals down and down until finally it opens out into a large hall. At first your attention is drawn to a long wooden table and you are struck with curiosity as to who would have sat in the now empty chairs. Then you become aware, beyond this table, of a huge golden presence. This is the spirit of the yew, an immensely wise and ancient being. You approach it and introduce yourself, all the while feeling honoured to be bathing in its golden presence.

Now make a request to the spirit of the yew that you would be immensely grateful to receive healing for your inner wounded child in order to release your inner magical child, so that you can then step onto the next spiral of your soul's evolution here on earth.

There to your left, an energetic time tunnel opens up and from it steps your inner wounded child—there may be one or several. These inner parts of your psyche are trapped in time, the eternal now of suffering, and are stressed and anxious. They come to you for safe haven. You scoop them up into your arms, and as you do so, a corridor of light appears and your spiritual ally motions for you to step into the light, which you do. Together with your animal ally and your inner children, you float up, supported by this stream of light. Up and up, up and up you go, until you find yourself in front of the gates of your very own magical garden, a place of peace and sanctuary, of rest and healing. The gates swing open and you step into the most beautiful garden you have ever seen, together with your animal ally and inner children. The scent is intoxicating and all of your favourite plants and trees enfold you with their colour, bathing you in their harmony. Take your time to really find yourself in your very own healing garden.

Then you become aware of a tall figure formed of bright white light and you know this to be your highest self. She steps forward and beckons for you and your inner wounded children to sit in a circle with her on the beautiful, soft green grass. She then passes around a talking stick and, as each child holds the talking stick in turn, they share their experiences in one word or many. Bear witness and hold sacred space for their experiences.

And now your highest self scoops up your inner children up onto her lap and embraces them in her healing white light of deep love and compassion, and you watch as they transform into giggling bundles of joy. They laugh, they dance, they sing, and you cannot resist joining in. And slowly they become one magical inner child—your inner child fully connected to Source and with an innate gift of manifesting your heart's desires, fully embracing life in wonder, awe and excitement. You are fully connected to your unique gifts and talents and fully connected to your reason for being here on earth at this exciting time of change.

Now it is time to leave. You embrace your highest self and she becomes one with you. Holding hands with your inner child and together with your animal ally, you make your way back through the gates, stepping into the corridor of light, down and down, down and down, back to the yew tree hall. The spirit of the yew steps forward and bestows a blessing upon you, your inner child and your animal ally. Feel this blessing now. Thank the spirit of the yew and turn round to embrace your inner magical child, and slowly feel yourself merging with her.

Then retrace your steps back up the spiral tunnel with your animal ally, up and up, up and up you go, until you step out of the gap in the trunk of the yew tree. Leave a gift for the tree at the foot of its trunk or, if it feels like you need to do something in your outer world then pledge this now.

Then travel back with your animal ally to the tree you started at, thanking it for accompanying you on your journey. Feel your feet on the ground, feel your fingers on the trunk. Gently opening your eyes, come back to your normal waking state.

A ROUNDING UP

I hope the information contained within this book has inspired you to try a different approach to gardening—one that will 'nurture your nature', as well as that of Mother Nature. Together we can start to repair the damage that we have done, born out of a disconnect to the web of life.

Connect with the spirit of your land, flow the green ray of Nature through you, call in Queen Maeve, the fae races and other beings of Nature, and begin to garden consciously.

Your land then becomes your temple space; conscious gardening becomes your active prayer/meditation and you will leave your garden re-enchanted with life.

Remember, you are Nature and we are all evolving back to the golden age of the 'One Heart'.*

Blessed be.

---

* Unity consciousness.

RESOURCES

The Art of Mindful Gardening by Ark Redwood (Leaping Hare Press, 2011)

The Book Of Stones by Robert Simmons and Naisha Ahsian (North Atlantic Books, 2015)

Conscious Gardening by Michael J Roads (Six Degrees Publishing Group, 2011)

Dancing with Nemetona by Joanna van der Hoeven (Moon Books, 2014)

The Earth's Cycle Of Celebration by Glennie Kindred (self-published, 1992)

Intuitive Herbalism by Nathaniel Hughes & Fiona Owen (Quintessence Press, 2014)

Letting in the Wild Edges by Glennie Kindred (Permanent Publications, 2013)

Messages From Nature's Guardians by Fiona Murray (Ribble Press, 2009)

Natural Gardening in Small Spaces by Noel Kingsbury (Timber Press, 2003)

Nature Spirits and Elemental Beings by Marko Pogačnik (Findhorn Press, 1996)

Nature Spirits, The Remembrance by Susan Raven (Clairview Books, 2012)

Plant Spirit Healing by Pam Montgomery (Bear & Company, 2008)

Plants that Speak, Souls that Sing by Fay Johnstone (Findhorn Press, 2018)

The Real World Of Faeries by Dora Van Gelder (Theosophical Publishing House, 1977)

The Sacred Tree by Glennie Kindred (self-published, 2003)

The Sensory Herbal Handbook by the Seed Sistas (Watkins Publishing, 2019)

The Sidhe by John Matthews, published by (Lorian Press, 2004)

Silver Wheel by Elen Tompkins (Head of Zeus, 2016)

The Spirit Of Trees by Fred Hageneder (Floris Books, 2000)

Weeds in the Heart by Nathaniel Hughes & Fiona Owen (Aeon Books, 2018)

Websites:

www.dragonwisdomschool.org

www.elementalbeings.co.uk

www.foxleas.com (information on plants, pollinating insects and gardening)

www.georgelizos.com

calistaascension.com

www.moonphasestudio.co.uk (sells an astrological moon planting calender)

www.noels-garden.blogspot.com (Noel Kingsbury writes many books on relaxed gardening, perennial planting and low-maintenance gardening using self-seeding plants. He also runs an online course: Planting Design With Perennials. 'Perennials are at the heart of a planting style which is naturalistic, sustainable and lower maintenance than most others).'

www.rhs.org.uk/plants-for-pollinators

www.rosybee.com Stocks (pollinator friendly plants)

www.wlgf.org (wildlife gardening forum)

Books to challenge C *your perception of reality*

A message from Clairview

We are an independent publishing company with a focus on cutting-edge, non-fiction books. Our innovative list covers current affairs and politics, health, the arts, history, science and spirituality. But regardless of subject, our books have a common link: they all question conventional thinking, dogmas and received wisdom.

Despite being a small company, our list features some big names, such as Booker Prize winner Ben Okri, literary giant Gore Vidal, world leader Mikhail Gorbachev, modern artist Joseph Beuys and natural childbirth pioneer Michel Odent.

So, check out our full catalogue online at
www.clairviewbooks.com
and join our emailing list for news on new titles.

office@clairviewbooks.com

CLAIRVIEW